PRESENTED TO

_____

FROM

A Story of God

and All of Us

REFLECTIONS

Roma Downey & Mark Burnett

New York | Boston | Nashville

For Reilly, James, and Cameron

All Scriptures are taken from the *Holy Bible, New International Version*®. Copyright © 1973, 1979, 1984, Biblica. Used by permission of Zondervan. All rights reserved.

Photography by Joe Albas and Casey Crawford and special thanks to Bob Beltz and Mishy Turner.

Editorial and design: Koechel Peterson & Associates, Inc., Minneapolis, Minnesota.

FaithWords
Hachette Book Group
237 Park Avenue
New York, NY 10017
www.faithwords.com

Printed in the United States of America

First Edition: February 2013

10 9 8 7 6 5 4 3

FaithWords is a division of Hachette Book Group, Inc.

The FaithWords name and logo are trademarks of Hachette Book Group, Inc.

The Hachette Speakers Bureau provides a wide range of authors for speaking events. To find out more, go to www.hachettespeakersbureau.com or call (866) 376-6591.

The publisher is not responsible for websites (or their content) that are not owned by the publisher.

ISBN: 978-1-4555-2567-6

Library of Congress Control Number: 2012954914

In the beginning

God created

the heavens and the earth.

GENESIS 1:1

$\mathcal{T}$hese are the opening words of the greatest book the world has ever known: the Bible. Several years ago, we decided to bring this story to the world in dramatic form. Why? Because there is a God, and he is real. He is the Creator, and he has spoken. We can know him! Everyone deserves to be told the story, to be inspired by it, to be touched by it—it is the story of God and all of us.

The word for *Bible* simply means "book." But this is THE book! It tells the story of God and his people—all of us! It proclaims that life has meaning and purpose. We are not simply the result of matter, time, and random cosmological events. God created the universe, life, and humanity. God created us because he loves us.

When you love someone, you want to communicate with them. Because God loves us, he wants to communicate with us. God speaks to us through the Bible. It is a compilation of those things God wants us to know about him, life, love, meaning, and purpose.

Our lives take on meaning when we open our hearts to God and enter into relationship with him. When that happens, spending consistent time with him is how we cultivate that relationship. We have put this devotional book together as a tool. We also hope you will see some of the deeper meaning behind the stories contained in *The Bible* series. Think of it as a love letter, in the same way the Bible is a love letter from God to all of us. May you remember today and every day, "God loves you." *Roma & Mark*

Father, thank you for loving us. We want to better understand how our lives are a part of your plan. We open our hearts to you. Thank you for giving us the Bible. We are grateful that you have left us such a great treasure through which you can speak to us. Help us experience your love and presence today. Amen.

> "Be still, and know that I am God."
>
> PSALM 46:10

I need regular quiet times in my life. The world is so noisy. Between the TV, computers, and mobile phones, it is hard to do what God tells us to do in today's verse. *Be still.* For me, that means finding some quiet space. It is in the quiet space that I hear God speak.

I try to take time daily to wait, listen, and feel. For most of us, God's voice doesn't come as a burning bush experience. At times, I wish it did. I've often wished "Monica" could show up for me, like I did for all those people on *Touched by an Angel.* It usually isn't that clear.

And yet, if we really have the ears to hear and eyes to see, God's voice is strong. Over time, you learn to know and hear it. As Mark and I worked on *The Bible* series, we prayed every day that we would have access to that knowing. We prayed that God would bring us the right people, and that he would provide solutions to challenges we faced. We watched and listened carefully.

When we are still, we are to know that God is God. That requires trust. We have learned to trust God. We had to trust him when the journey of *The Bible* began, and we learned to trust him throughout the process. It has deepened our spiritual journey.

We are glad that you are reading these devotional thoughts. For you, this might be your quiet time and space. We hope that you will seek to hear the voice of God speaking to you through what you read. And we pray that as you learn to listen, you will grow in your confidence that he is God. He loves you and wants to be part of your life today and every day.

 R

Heavenly Father, help us take time to get alone with you in a quiet place. Teach us to hear you when you speak. You speak through the Bible. You speak by your Spirit. You have created us with the capacity to hear your voice. Help us be still so we can know you and hear you in our hearts. Guide us and help us trust in you. Amen.

Every good and perfect gift is from above,
coming down from the Father of the
heavenly lights, who does not change
like shifting shadows.

JAMES 1:17

We consider our love and our children to be among the good gifts God has given us. Our story is a beautiful example of how God works when you pray for his will in your life.

We had both met with disappointment in relationships before. We came to a point where we needed God's help and wisdom in meeting and choosing a life partner. I asked God to choose for me. I actually made a list of suggestions for God! I wrote out the qualities that were important to me and then handed them over to God to find a husband who would be my soul mate, my lover, my best friend, and life partner.

I did ask God to let me know when my answered prayer was here. I knew God would send him, but I wanted to make sure I recognized him when he arrived! God sent Mark. I knew he was the answer. Just to make sure, I introduced Mark to Della Reese. In classic Della fashion, she put Mark through his paces and then came and told me, "Baby girl, he is the one!"

I don't know what you need in your life. Sometimes it is hard to distinguish needs from wants. But I know God has good gifts for you. I'm sure he has already given you many. But ask him for what he wants for you. Turn your needs over to him and ask for his best. Trust his love for you. Ask him not to give you anything that would *not* be good for you. Trust his timing—it is always perfect. And always be sure to give him thanks for every good and perfect gift he bestows! *R*

> Heavenly Father, thank you for all your good gifts
> in our lives. Help us seek what you desire for our
> lives. Teach us how to pray in a way that releases the
> treasures of heaven. Thank you for your greatest and
> most loving gift: Jesus. Amen.

When the woman saw that the fruit
of the tree was good for food and pleasing
to the eye, and also desirable for gaining wisdom,
she took some and ate it.

GENESIS 3:6

DO NOT MERELY LISTEN TO THE WORD,

and so deceive yourselves.

DO WHAT IT SAYS.

JAMES 1:22

*W*hen we read the Bible thoughtfully, with an open heart and mind, or hear it being taught or preached with the same openness, God will speak to us. The Holy Spirit uses the Bible as a means through which God communicates directly with us. When we sense God is speaking to us, it is important that we respond to what he is saying! Hear and respond. That is the intended pattern. James says that if there is not a response, we are deceiving ourselves about having authentic faith.

Information is not the only purpose of the Bible. It is intended to produce transformation. Transformation requires actually doing the things God's Word teaches us.

We encourage you to take some time today and get away to a quiet place. Read the Bible. If you don't know where to start, try reading the chapter in James from which today's verse is taken. Ask God to speak to you. If you sense him speaking through the text, ask what you need to do to respond. Then do it! ✐ *M*

Heavenly Father, help us hear your Word.
Make the Bible come alive and use it to speak to us.
Teach us what you would have us do. Give us grace
and strength through your Spirit to put into practice
the things you teach us.
Amen.

> Do not conform any longer to the pattern of this world, but be transformed by the renewing of your mind. Then you will be able to test and approve what God's will is—his good, pleasing and perfect will.
>
> ROMANS 12:2

I love butterflies. A friend once told me that they are "the wink of God." I can't begin to tell you how often, just when I needed a little encouragement, God sent a butterfly. We even had butterfly designs woven into the arbor we stood under when we exchanged our wedding vows. They have a special significance to us.

Butterflies also have a big lesson to teach us. God is in the business of transformation. The word *metamorphosis* is actually derived from a Greek word Paul uses in today's verse. The process of spiritual transformation is not unlike a caterpillar's transformation into a butterfly.

I once heard a story of a young child who found a caterpillar's cocoon with a butterfly struggling to emerge from it. In an attempt to help the butterfly, the child ran into the house and found a tiny pair of scissors with which the child cut the remaining part of the cocoon to free the butterfly. What the child couldn't have known is that the struggle of emerging from the cocoon is a critical part of the process that enables the butterfly to fly. In attempting to ease the struggle, the child had accidentally ruined the process of metamorphosis.

I've found the same to be true in my life. When I face challenge and difficulty, I want God to rescue me and free me from the struggle. But sometimes it is the very difficulty that we are trying to overcome that gives us strength to fly. This is our metamorphosis and how we become strong. Next time you are struggling, pray that God would send a butterfly to remind you he loves you and is transforming your life to make you stronger—so you can spread your wings and soar. 𝒪ℛ

Heavenly Father, thank you for all the times you send "butterflies" into our lives to let us know you are there and you care. When we are in times of struggle, help us remember that you use these things to make us into the kind of people you created us to be—strong and with wings to soar. We love you and praise your name. Amen.

I am my lover's and my lover is mine . . .

SONG OF SOLOMON 6:3

I have an amazing wife. We met while both living in California. A friendship turned into a romance, and a romance into deep love. We both had a growing sense that God had brought us together. On a moonlit night in Zihuatanejo, Mexico, on a torch-lit beach, we became engaged.

The words of today's verse are words that reflect our commitment to each other. I am Roma's, and she is mine. She is my beloved. Marriage is used in the Bible as a metaphor for our relationship with God. Some scholars believe that the importance of today's verse is that it symbolically reflects the intimacy of relationship we should have with God. I like that thought.

I love God. He loves me. He doesn't just want me to know about him. He wants me to know *about* him. I knew a great deal about Roma before we met. Both of our series were currently on CBS. I had watched episodes of *Touched by an Angel* and admired her gentleness, and although beautiful, she exuded grace and humility. We had only met in passing at TV events. And when I met her, I wanted to know her, personally. I wanted to have a relationship. And eventually I wanted to spend the rest of my life with her.

This is what God desires for each of us. He is ready and willing. It is up to us to reach out and begin to know him. *M*

Father, I am amazed at the magnitude of your love.
I want to know you better. I want to love you more.
Help me grow my love of you. Amen.

But Noah found favor
in the eyes of the LORD.

GENESIS 6:8

So we fix our eyes not on what is seen, but on what is unseen. For what is seen is temporary, but what is unseen is eternal.

2 CORINTHIANS 4:18

For some people the journey of life can be long and hard, the road is stormy, and they have burdens to carry that few could ever manage. Dreams have been lost, loved ones have passed away, bills outnumber paychecks, and challenges outweigh strength. It's easy to feel tired and discouraged and hard to see the light at the end of the journey. You want to go on, but some days the road just seems too long and too dark. But be encouraged. God never said that the road would be easy, but he did say that the light at the end of the road would shine brightly and that the arrival would be worthwhile. ✍ *ROM*

Dear Father, we know that no matter how long or bumpy the road may seem that you are with us every step we take. You bring light out of darkness, and for this we are always grateful. Amen.

Blessed is the man who does not walk in the counsel of the wicked or stand in the way of sinners or sit in the seat of mockers. But his delight is in the law of the LORD, and on his law he meditates day and night.

PSALM 1:1–2

You might think of the Book of Psalms as containing "God's Greatest Hits." The words of the psalms are actually lyrics to songs that were sung in the Temple in Jerusalem when the people came to worship. David, the king of Israel, wrote about half of the psalms contained in the Bible. The first psalm is actually about the Bible itself. The words poetically describe how our engagement with the Scriptures can produce a life of prosperity.

These lyrics say that prosperity is the result of avoiding bad counsel and delighting in the truth contained in the Bible. As David paints a brief picture of the person who is prosperous, he notes that this is someone who meditates on the truth of the Bible day and night.

It is important to remember that prosperity from God's perspective is not the same as the idea of prosperity in our modern culture. In biblical terms, the idea is much more about living a life of meaning and purpose. It carries the sense of being successful in experiencing God's plans and purposes for our lives.

God wants us to prosper. He wants us to discover and successfully live out his reason for creating us. He wants us to live blessed lives. To that end, he has given us the Bible. As we read the Bible and meditate on it throughout the day, we allow the truth we discover to guide our day; then we will prosper! *M*

Father, thank you for the Bible. Thank you for the great truths contained in the psalms, and the beautiful way they are expressed. Help me today to think and pray and meditate on your Word. Help me live a life that is pleasing to you. Amen.

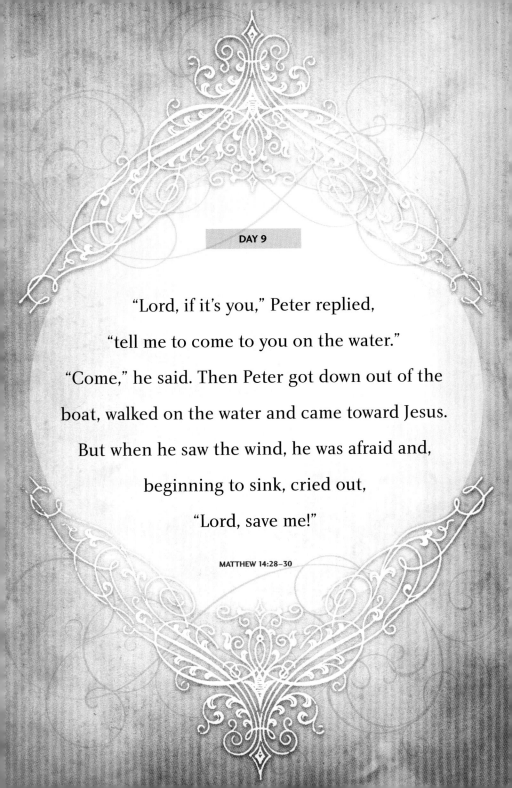

"Lord, if it's you," Peter replied,

"tell me to come to you on the water."

"Come," he said. Then Peter got down out of the

boat, walked on the water and came toward Jesus.

But when he saw the wind, he was afraid and,

beginning to sink, cried out,

"Lord, save me!"

MATTHEW 14:28–30

*W*e live by the ocean; we have always been drawn to it. We find it calming as well as beautiful. The tides roll in and out; the constant ebb and flow of the waves is like a massage of the mind and of the spirit.

Living by the sea opens our hearts as well, as the scale of the ocean reminds us of God's love. It's just so big.

Recently a girlfriend of mine came to visit and took her little boy to the beach. She was expecting him to be overjoyed and exhilarated by the waves, but the ocean terrified him. He was overcome and could not stop crying. He wouldn't even put his feet in the sand, and he would not go anywhere near the water's edge. "I am scared," he said, "because the ocean is so big and I am so small."

The truth is there have been some days since we began work on *The Bible* series when this work just feels so BIG and we feel so small. We feel unworthy, filled with self-doubt, and fearful we will be swept away and drown in failure or criticism. We feel small, anxious, and sometimes it even makes us take our eyes off of what is real and true. Reality gets distorted.

That's what happened to Peter. For a moment, he was walking on water, literally walking on water; then doubt seeped in, and he became afraid and began to sink. We love this biblical story because Peter is so human, so like us. Peter is bold and willing to take risks on the one hand, and fearful and full of doubt on the other. He shows us what it means to be caught midway between faith and doubt.

Someone sent me a tweet recently that I just loved: "When you feel like you are drowning in the sea of your life, remember that your lifeguard walks on water!" I LOVE THAT.

Jesus told Peter, "Take courage! It is I. Don't be afraid." *M R*

Dear God, please help us to have courage and trust in you, for your love is deeper than the ocean and wider than the sea. You are BIGGER than fear and doubt. You are always there for us. Amen.

"You should not be surprised at my saying, 'You must be born again.' The wind blows wherever it pleases. You hear its sound, but you cannot tell where it comes from or where it is going. So it is with everyone born of the Spirit."

JOHN 3:7–8

One of the more amazing experiences that happened on the set of *The Bible* took place as we were filming the scene from which today's verses are taken. We felt the hand of God on the project from the beginning, but this was special. It happened as we were filming the scene in which the Jewish Pharisee Nicodemus came at night to visit Jesus. This scene takes place in episode 8.

It was early evening, and we were around a campfire filming the scene. Nicodemus had just arrived, and Jesus lovingly welcomed him into the camp. It was a warm evening, and the air was still and calm. The two sat down together by the fire. Jesus spoke to Nicodemus of the need to be born again by the Spirit. He then spoke the words about the Spirit being like the wind blowing where it pleases. Suddenly, as if on cue, the wind began to blow. It whisked through the campfire and swirled up where tree branches and leaves began swaying and rustling. Even Jesus' hair began to blow about. It was extraordinary.

It took the entire crew's breath away. There had been zero wind, and then, as if on cue, it moved through the camp. We could not have timed it more perfectly. It was clearly a divine moment where God was saying, "I am here!"

Our experience reflected what Jesus said to Nicodemus. The work of the Holy Spirit is mysterious. We can't always see what God is up to, but we often see the results. He is at work in your life at this very moment. You might not feel it. You might not believe it. But it is still true. *R&M*

Heavenly Father, thank you for the gift of spiritual life. Thank you that when you invade our lives with your Holy Spirit, we experience new birth. We open our hearts to you. Let the wind of your Spirit blow where it will today. Amen.

An anxious heart weighs a man down,
but a kind word cheers him up.

PROVERBS 12:25

I was raised in Ireland. My mother passed away when I was a little girl, and my father stepped into the role of both parents. He was a quiet man, filled with integrity, love, and kindness. He was the kindest person I knew. He was a man filled with faith. Through my childhood, he would take time to pray with me. We would pray together in our little kitchen with the sound of the rain on the windows outside.

When I finished high school, with his blessing, I went to college in England. I was homesick and missed him dearly. I had a trip planned to return to Ireland and spoke to my dad the night before to finalize my travel plans. I was so excited to see him. "It's been raining here and is damp," he said, "so I've hung your favorite yellow flannel sheets on the indoor clothesline to air." He was so kind and thoughtful. I went to sleep knowing I was loved and excited about getting home the next day. But the unexpected happened. In the middle of the night, my father had a heart attack and died.

I went home on the same flight and arrived at my home, heartbroken and devastated. I walked into our little kitchen, and there hanging on the indoor clothesline to air were my favorite yellow flannel sheets. Kindness, his last loving act of kindness. I took them in my hands and breathed in his love. His kindness touched me. I felt his love. And all these years later, I still do. Just as I feel the love of my dad, I feel the love of my heavenly Father—forever looking after me and forever loving me. *R*

Dear Father, we thank you for the gifts of kindness
in our lives, for the kindness and love that others
show to us and that we in return show to others.
You taught us to love, Jesus, saying "love one another
as I have loved you." Let us always remember this,
and remind us to be kind whenever it is possible.
Help us to see it is always possible to be kind, to do
good for others in your name. In Jesus' name we pray.
Amen.

*A*bram believed the LORD,

and he credited it to him as righteousness.

GENESIS 15:6

ONE DAY JESUS WAS PRAYING

in a certain place. When he finished,

one of his disciples said to him,

"LORD, TEACH US TO PRAY,

just as John taught his disciples."

LUKE 11:1

*T*he Lord's Prayer plays a special role in my spiritual life. My primary means of staying in shape is cycling. I love riding my bike on the hills in Southern California. As I ride, I pray the words Jesus taught his disciples when they made the request contained in today's verse. I love this scene in episode 7 of our series.

Now, as I pray, I pause and think about what each phrase means. I've discovered that you can use the prayer as a tool to lead you in praying about the various issues Jesus addresses. There is a certain pattern to it.

When I pray, "Our Father who art in heaven," I think and pray about my relationship with God as our loving Father and try to imagine God embracing me as a father. When I pray, "Give us this day our daily bread," I think about our scene at the "feeding of the 5,000," when Jesus explains that "if God feeds the birds of the air, how much more will he give to you." Then I pray about the needs in my life for that day. When I pray, "Forgive us our trespasses," I pause and think about anything in my life that I need to get honest with God about. Each phrase is a "trigger" that helps me pray as I ride. As you read through the prayer today, pause after each phrase and see what comes to your mind. Respond to God in prayer about these thoughts:

Our Father in heaven, *(he is our Father)*
Hallowed be your name. *(God is almighty)*
Your kingdom come, your will be done
On earth as it is in heaven. *(turn your life over to him)*
Give us this day our daily bread. *(realize God will*
    meet your need and then pray about your needs)
Forgive us our trespasses, as we forgive those who
have trespassed against us.
    (know you are forgiven as soon as you forgive others)
Lead us not into temptation, but deliver us from evil.
    (protection for the day)
For yours is the kingdom, and the power,
    and the glory forever. Amen.

For out of
the overflow
of his heart
his mouth
speaks.

LUKE 6:45

What are you talking about these days? Is there any particular subject that dominates your conversation? Are you talking about substantive issues or mostly chattering away? There is often an emphasis on making sure our actions validate our language, but how about considering that our language reveals the true state of our hearts?

Today's text seems to infer that what comes out of our mouths reveals something about what is really going on deep inside us. Immediately preceding today's text, Jesus teaches that "the good man brings good things out of the good stored up in his heart," while "the evil man brings evil things out of the evil stored up in his heart."

As you engage in conversation today, think about what you hear coming out of the mouths of those around you. Consider that their language reveals something about who they really are. Then turn the focus back on yourself. Be conscious of what you talk about and how you do it. What does your language reveal about your heart?

Dear God, as we speak today, fill us with your love so that our words may reveal fullness in our hearts. Take away fear, take away negative chatter, O loving Father. We speak out in praise of your name. Amen.

Bear with each other and forgive whatever
grievances you may have against one another.
Forgive as the Lord forgave you.

COLOSSIANS 3:13

Nearly everyone has been hurt by the actions or words of others. We know that sometimes these wounds can leave you with lasting feelings of anger or bitterness. But if you don't practice forgiveness, you might be the one who pays most dearly. By embracing forgiveness, you can also embrace peace, hope, gratitude, and joy.

We can pray for the Holy Spirit to strengthen us to make this decision to let go of resentment. The act that hurt or offended us might always remain a part of our lives, but forgiveness can lessen its grip on you and help you focus on other more positive and loving parts of your life. Forgiveness can lead to feelings of understanding, empathy, and compassion for the one who hurt you. Amazing grace. With God, all things are possible.

You can forgive the person without excusing the act. But forgiveness does bring a kind of peace that helps you get on with your life. When we let go of the anger, God's love can be very healing.

 R&M

Our Father in heaven, we pray today . . .
forgive us our trespasses as we forgive those
who trespass against us. Lord, please soften
our hearts so that we may be healed through
your grace and your love. Help us to let go
of the old hurts that only hold us back,
and as we are able to let go of these hurts,
fill our hearts with your love and compassion.
Amen.

*S*arah became pregnant and bore a son
to Abraham in his old age, at the very time
God had promised him. Abraham gave the name
Isaac to the son Sarah bore him.

GENESIS 21:2–3

Abraham answered,

"God himself will provide

the lamb for the burnt offering, my son."

GENESIS 22:8

And if you spend yourselves on behalf of
the hungry and satisfy the needs of the oppressed,
then your light will rise in the darkness,
and your night will become like the noonday.
The Lord will guide you always; he will satisfy your
needs in a sun-scorched land and will strengthen
your frame. You will be like a well-watered garden,
like a spring whose waters never fail.

ISAIAH 58:10–11

*W*henever I was feeling blue as a teenager, my father would encourage me to remember to be considerate of other people—to step up in the service of others. He always said that not only was it the right thing to do, but helping others can help get your attention away from your own problems. Sometimes we can feel as if we're in a hole, and we can't find a way out. By stepping up and helping others, we can break this cycle and open our hearts. The love, compassion, and acceptance we show to others puts our faith into action and often comes back to us in healing and joy.

Our hearts long for fulfillment, and we can find this through loving service of others.

In Matthew 25:40, the Scripture says, "I tell you the truth, whatever you did for one of the least of these brothers of mine, you did for me." We are reminded to see the face of Christ in every single person we meet and to step up into loving kindness. When we connect with the endless well of love in our own hearts, we are like a well-watered garden with God's love as the source. This love is a spring inside of us, endless and never failing, a well-watered garden blooming in the abundance of God's love. *R*

Dear Father, we thank you for your abundant love. We know you are the source of all love. Help us to remember to see you in everyone we meet today. And through our kind actions and loving words, others may know you. Amen.

The LORD said to Moses, "Tell Aaron and his sons, 'This is how you are to bless the Israelites. Say to them: "'The LORD bless you and keep you; the LORD make his face shine on you . . .'"'"

NUMBERS 6:22–25

We consider ourselves blessed. We actually consider ourselves to be *greatly* blessed. We are grateful to God for all he has done in our lives. Our greatest blessings are our love for each other, our sense of God's love for us, and the beautiful children he has given us. We have grown in our appreciation that all we have is a gift from a loving God.

God is in the "blessing business." His first act in relationship to Adam and Eve was to bless them. His call to Abraham included a promise that God would bless him so that he could be a blessing. In today's verses, God gives Moses instructions on how Aaron and the Jewish priesthood were to be instruments through whom God's blessing could be given to the entire nation of Israel. In church, we often hear these verses used as a closing benediction.

We desire to be instruments of God's blessing in the world. That was one of our major motivations for producing *The Bible* series. We wanted you to be blessed. We also desire that you be a blessing to others. This is God's plan for the entire world. It requires us to stay in a dynamic relationship with him on a daily basis, so that he can fill us with his presence. When we experience God's love, we will be blessed. We then become vehicles for his love to others; they will be blessed. As was true of Abraham, we will be blessed to be a blessing.

Ask God to bless you today, and ask him to make you an instrument of his blessing. We believe God will always answer this prayer! *R&M*

Heavenly Father, thank you that you are the source of all blessing in our lives. Bless us today. We ask this not only for ourselves, but so that we can be a blessing in the lives of all we come in contact with today and every day. Amen.

*"Ah, Sovereign LORD," I said, "I do not know
how to speak; I am only a child."
But the LORD said to me, "Do not say,
'I am only a child.' You must go to everyone
I send you to and say whatever I command you.
Do not be afraid of them,
for I am with you and will rescue you,"
declares the LORD.*

JEREMIAH 1:6–8

We know exactly how Jeremiah felt. We have never been more challenged than in producing *The Bible* series. It is the most exciting project we have ever been involved in, and at times we both have felt the sense of inadequacy to do justice to God's Word that Jeremiah expresses in today's verses. Jeremiah plays a central role in the last episode of the Old Testament.

Today's verses contain part of God's call on the life of Jeremiah to be his prophet. He was a prophet during one of the most critical times in Israel's history. His message was not an easy one. From the world's perspective, he must have appeared to be a complete failure. No one listened to the message God sent through him. But from God's perspective, he was faithful, and thus a complete success.

That is what we hope we can be. We want to be faithful to God's call on our lives. We believe everyone's purpose in life is to be instruments of God's plans and purposes. We can spend our lives doing many other things, but if we want to find the kind of meaning our hearts long for, we need to discover and do the will of God.

When we seek to do what we think God is telling us to do, he is with us. He can work through us, and he can use us. If you don't know what God wants you to do today, ask him. Then listen to your heart. You might be surprised what begins to stir within it. *ROM*

Father, sometimes we feel inadequate to be used
by you. We feel like Jeremiah. Thank you that
you are the one who works through us and enables
us to do your will. Let us know your purpose and
strengthen us to do your will. Amen.

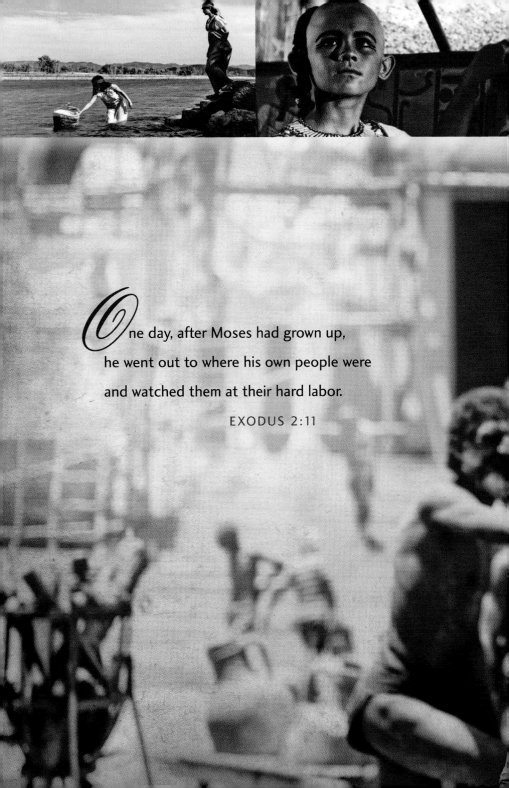

One day, after Moses had grown up,

he went out to where his own people were

and watched them at their hard labor.

EXODUS 2:11

"*W*ho am I, that I should go to Pharaoh and bring the Israelites out of Egypt?"

EXODUS 3:11

Praise the LORD,
O my soul,
and forget not
all his benefits.

PSALM 103:2

Today is a new day. Whatever you may be facing today, don't forget that God wants to satisfy you with good things. Do not forget his benefits. If you have made mistakes in your life, forgiveness is a benefit. If you feel overwhelmed or overworked or tired, strength is a benefit. If you need healing today, that healing is a benefit. God will bestow benefits on you that will strengthen and empower you to overcome any obstacle that you have in your life.

Today is a new day. Remember that God is amazing and that through Him all things are possible.

RDM

Heavenly Father, we thank you for all of your goodness. We take none of these benefits for granted. You are loving and gracious. We praise your name and accept your gifts with graceful hearts. Today is a new day to love you. Amen.

When Moses' hands grew tired, they took a
stone and put it under him and he sat on it.
Aaron and Hur held his hands up—
one on one side, one on the other—
so that his hands remained steady till sunset.

EXODUS 17:12

Everyone needs a couple of good friends in their life to stand with them when the battle gets tough. Today's verse gives us a great picture of how much we need one another.

Moses had sent Joshua to lead the army of Israel onto the field of battle against their enemies. Moses went to a nearby hill to hold the staff of God over the battle, so that God would fight on behalf of his people. Fortunately, he also took Aaron and Hur with him. As long as Moses held the staff up high, the army of Israel prevailed. If he lowered the staff, the enemy gained the advantage.

Moses wasn't a superhero. His arms got tired. That's when Hur and Aaron came up with a strategy. They put a rock under Moses so he could sit, and each of them took one of Moses' arms and held it up. Joshua fought the battle till sunset and defeated the enemy. What a great picture of how we can win the battles we face!

We all face battles that we can't fight by ourselves. There are a lot of times when we need a few good friends to help us fight. Similar to Moses, our "hands grow tired." That's when we need our friends to come alongside and hold them up! In our marriage, we are so grateful to have each other, because we can take turns holding each other up when needed. God uses us to help each other. We hope you have an "Aaron" and a "Hur" in your life *R&M*

Father, thank you for the people you bring into our lives that help us when the battle gets to be more than we can handle by ourselves. Help us invest in friendships that are like the ones Moses had. Help us be like Aaron and Hur in the lives of our friends. Father, remind us that when we struggle, you are always there with us, holding us in your loving arms. Amen.

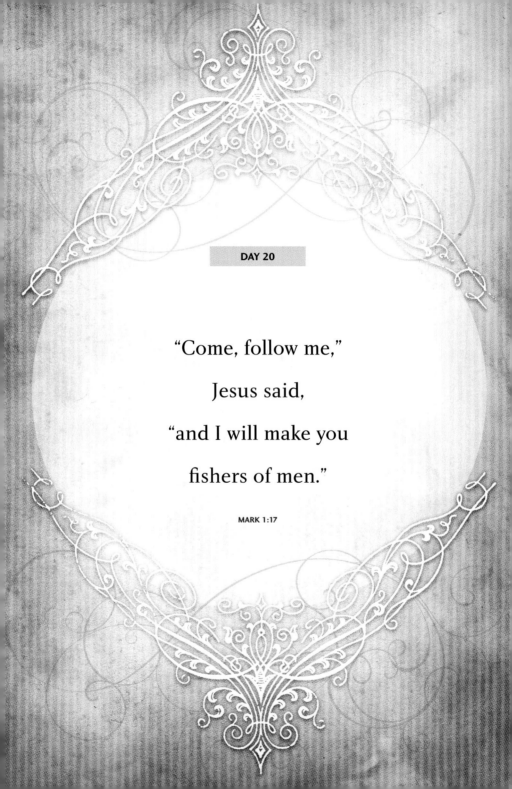

"Come, follow me,"

Jesus said,

"and I will make you

fishers of men."

MARK 1:17

As we worked on the script for *The Bible*, we wanted to include a scene of this moment when Jesus called Peter to a new life. As we filmed the scene, we imagined what it may have been like to be at Capernaum when Jesus and Peter headed out to deep water on the Sea of Galilee to go fishing. We love the way our writers gave fresh meaning to Jesus' invitation for Peter to become a fisher of men. Peter asks what they are going to do, and Jesus replies, "Change the world!"

Although this invitation by Jesus was issued to his first-century disciples, this is an invitation that is offered to us daily. Every day we have the opportunity to seek God's will for our lives and then attempt to do it. For us, the sense of call to make *The Bible* was just such a moment. God desires our relationship with him to be vital and dynamic. He wants us to hear him calling, "Come, follow me."

Living near the ocean, we have the joy of walking along the beach, much as Jesus and his friends were able to do in Capernaum. We have often reflected on how there is an immense difference between making a living and truly experiencing life. Peter knew how to make a living, but he was about to find out what it meant to have a life.

We have been blessed in our lives. But we can truly say that only those things that God has called us to do have brought deep fulfillment. We are grateful for the sense of God's love and presence in our lives. We pray you experience his love and presence also. *R@M*

Heavenly Father, thank you for your great love.
Without your love, we will never know true life.
Thank you that we can know you and experience
your love. Lord, help us today to hear your call to
"Come, follow me!" Amen.

"FOR GOD SO LOVED THE WORLD

that he gave his one and only Son,

THAT WHOEVER BELIEVES IN HIM

shall not perish but have eternal life."

JOHN 3:16

$\mathcal{T}$his is the most well-known Bible verse in the world. It is one of our favorites as well. In my career as an actress, I am probably most known for my role as Monica on *Touched by an Angel*. For almost ten years on a weekly basis, I had the joy of delivering the message, "God loves you." I imagine the reason John 3:16 is the most well-known verse in the Bible, and also the most loved verse, is because it clearly expresses the words I had the privilege of communicating.

If there is one unifying thought with which we wanted to permeate *The Bible*, it is this reality that God loves every person on the face of the Earth. God so loved the world that he gave his one and only Son.

We hope that people will experience the truth of God's love through *The Bible* series. It is the message that motivates us in all we do. They are words that inspire and strengthen us, encourage and raise us up. We pray that as you read this devotional day by day, you will hear these words and remember that God loves you. He so loved you that he gave his one and only Son. *R*

Heavenly Father, thank you for your love.
We marvel that you loved us enough to send Jesus.
We are so grateful that as we open our lives to you,
you pour your love into our hearts. Help us experience
your love today and every day. Amen.

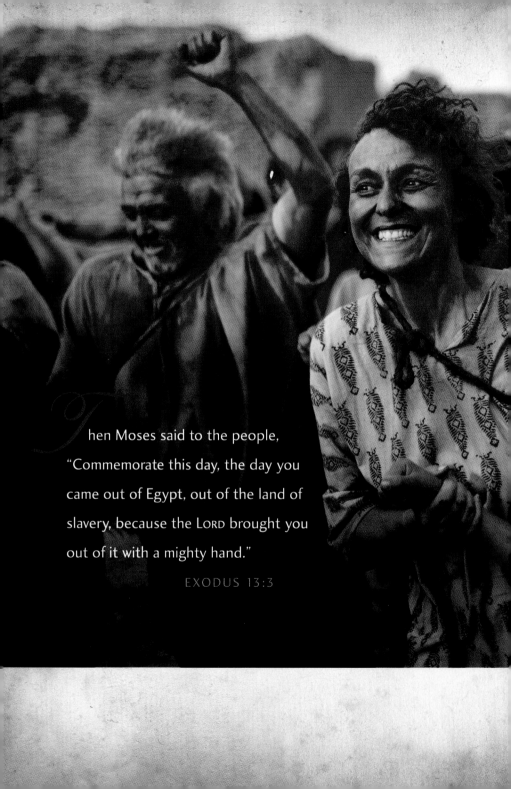

Then Moses said to the people, "Commemorate this day, the day you came out of Egypt, out of the land of slavery, because the LORD brought you out of it with a mighty hand."

EXODUS 13:3

DAY 22

The LORD is my shepherd,

I shall not be in want.

He makes me lie down in green pastures,

he leads me beside quiet waters,

he restores my soul.

PSALM 23:1–3

The twenty-third psalm is my favorite. I remember my father reading it to me as a child. I could always imagine a beautiful field of green grass with a brilliant blue stream slowly flowing through the middle of it. At times I could picture myself running and playing in the field, and even picture Jesus being there with me. And there were butterflies! I love butterflies. They are some of the most beautiful creatures our loving heavenly Father created. Sometimes, I think he created them just for me. Whenever I see one, it is as if he is sending me the message, "I am here."

Throughout my life, the Lord has been my Shepherd. In filming episode 3 of *The Bible*, we see David looking for his sheep. Watching the scene unfold, seeing how he tended to them, guided them, and protected them, made me think of how God has shown his love for me.

The Lord has provided for me. My life has been blessed. I have a husband and three beautiful children who enrich my life beyond description. I am blessed because the Lord is my Shepherd.

When I look back on my journey, the places I have been, the opportunities I have had, and the people I have met, I see the hand of God at work in the design of my life. Looking back, I see the Lord guiding me, loving me, and taking care of me.

The Lord has protected me. My life has not been without challenges and difficulty. But when danger threatened, God protected me. When I experienced loss, God comforted me. I have felt his love and protection my whole life. The Lord is indeed my Shepherd.

The Lord wants to be involved in your life. If you seek him, he will be your Shepherd, as he has been for me.

Heavenly Father, thank you that you are our Shepherd. Thank you for your provision, your guidance, and your protection in our lives. Shepherd us today and every day. If ever we get lost, please come and find us and lead us home. Amen.

"WHERE YOU GO I WILL GO,

and where you stay I will stay.

YOUR PEOPLE WILL BE MY PEOPLE

and your God my God."

RUTH 1:16

By the time I finished college, I was an orphan. My mother had died when I was ten, and my father died while I was away at school. Their deaths created a great void in my life and a yearning for the love that only a parent can give. Then I met Della. We met on the set of *Touched by an Angel* and have been an important part of each other's lives ever since. We were fast friends from day one, but the relationship took a major turn in the middle of those years.

Della's daughter died during our time filming the series. It was a painful loss to her, in the same way the death of my mother was to me. Not long after, Della took me in her arms and said, "God is so amazing, baby, because I always knew that he brought me into your life because you needed a momma. I just hadn't realized that he brought you into my life because I was going to need a baby girl." She said, "Will you be my baby?" I said, "Yes." She said, "Then I am your momma." From that day forward, she has been my mother. We are family. I love her, and she is my momma.

Today's verse is taken from a very similar event in the Bible. Naomi had lost both of her sons while living as an expatriate in Moab. She tried to send her young daughters-in-law away to find new husbands, and she planned to return to Israel. But Ruth would not leave her. In a beautiful expression of her love for Naomi, she spoke the words contained in today's verse.

Her love was so great that she became more than a daughter-in-law. She became a daughter to Ruth in the same way I became a daughter to Della. I am so grateful to Della for loving me. And I am so grateful to God for sending her to me, for restoring a mother's love to my life. God is good, and I am grateful. *R*

*Heavenly Father, thank you. I know that
one of the ways you express your love to us is through
the people you bring into our lives. We pray today that you
would help us see the ones who are your gifts to us
and love them with your love. We are grateful to you
for loving us the way you do. Amen.*

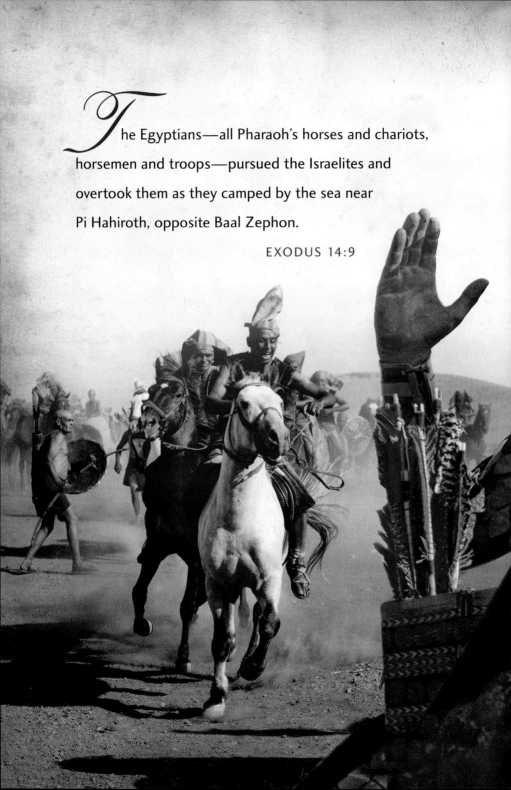

The Egyptians—all Pharaoh's horses and chariots, horsemen and troops—pursued the Israelites and overtook them as they camped by the sea near Pi Hahiroth, opposite Baal Zephon.

EXODUS 14:9

WHEN THE DAY OF PENTECOST CAME,

they were all together in one place.

SUDDENLY A SOUND LIKE THE BLOWING

of a violent wind came from heaven

and filled the whole house

where they were sitting.

ACTS 2:1–2

*M*ark and I had many moments on the set of *The Bible* when we felt God's presence. This was certainly the case as we filmed the Pentecost experience in episode 10. In the Bible, we read how the Holy Spirit came upon the disciples. There was the sound of a rushing wind. What appeared to be tongues of fire came to rest on the disciples. The Spirit filled them with his presence and the presence of Jesus.

The significance of this moment in the story is immense. It was the evidence that Jesus once more shared the glory of the Father. It fulfilled the promise Jesus made that he would send them the Helper, the Holy Spirit.

From this point forward, life for the followers of Jesus would be a process of the Spirit of God working through them. The same is true for all of us.

We can allow Jesus to live and love through us. What happened on the day of Pentecost can take place in all of our lives. All you have to do is ask. As you open your heart, the Spirit will come. Breathe, believe, and receive. *R*

Heavenly Father, as you did during Pentecost,
we ask you to send your Holy Spirit to live in us.
We pray you would live in us and love
through us today and every day.
Amen.

> If I speak in the tongues of men and of angels, but have not love, I am only a resounding gong or a clanging cymbal.
>
> 1 CORINTHIANS 13:1

I will always remember the day Mark and I stood under a beautiful arbor in the garden of our home where my dearest friend, Della Reese (an ordained minister), led us in the exchange of our wedding vows. That day, Mark and I pledged to love each other as husband and wife for the rest of our lives.

Today's verse was read as part of our wedding ceremony. The chapter from which it is taken is often called "the love chapter." It contains some of my favorite verses in the Bible.

Marriage requires a special kind of love. Love is more than a feeling. I like to say that love is action. Loving is a decision we make to treat another person as Jesus treated people. The "love chapter" gives a number of specific characteristics of this kind of love.

This kind of love is patient and kind. These are two of the qualities that Mark and I work at in our marriage. We need to be patient with each other, because it is inevitable that we will do and say things that make the other hurt or angry. There are times when I need to walk away from a fight and let things cool down. Love enables us to choose to act with patience even when we feel impatient.

Love is kind. Kindness is one of the greatest expressions of love. The love Paul writes about is unconditional. Sometimes, when my initial reaction is to be unkind, the loving response is to choose to be kind, even when that is not what I'm feeling. Only God can help you love like this. But he will. He has the ability to love in and through us, if we let him—if we open ourselves to him. *R*

Heavenly Father, teach me to be more loving today. Pour out your love in my heart and love through me. Help me choose to be patient and kind today to everyone you bring across my path. Help me to see you in everyone I meet today. Amen.

All scripture is God-breathed and is useful
for teaching, rebuking, correcting and training
in righteousness, so that the man of God may
be thoroughly equipped for every good work.

2 TIMOTHY 3:16–17

We love the way this version of the Scriptures uses the word *God-breathed* in today's verses. Most other English translations read "inspired." This is what true inspiration means: God-breathed. It conjures in our minds those days when we were filming *The Bible* and the desert winds of Morocco would come suddenly and without warning. Sometimes they came a little too strongly, turning our set into a dustbowl. But at other times, the wind seemed to be coming directly from God. It was as if the Spirit of God had chosen in that moment to make his presence known through the wind.

The Bible is "God-breathed." The human authors of the Bible became instruments in the hands of God, and he breathed into them. In some mysterious and mystical way, what came from their pens were the very words of God. St. Peter writes that they were "carried along by the Holy Spirit" (2 Peter 1:21). I can vividly picture in my mind the days when we were shooting the scenes portraying Jesus and the disciples in boats on the Sea of Galilee. I remember the sails of the boats being raised and suddenly the wind coming and carrying them across the water.

Because it is "inspired," the Bible is a book like no other. The God who inspired it can use it to speak to us directly. He uses his Spirit to illuminate the text and speak truth into our lives. He teaches us who he is, who we are, and how to live the way he intended us to live. When we read the Bible, we often sense that God breathes fresh life into us. We pray that as you read these words today, God would do the same to you. *M. R*

Heavenly Father, thank you that you are there
and that you have spoken to us. We marvel.
Speak your word to us today. Breathe your loving
Spirit into us that we may be inspired by you.
Amen.

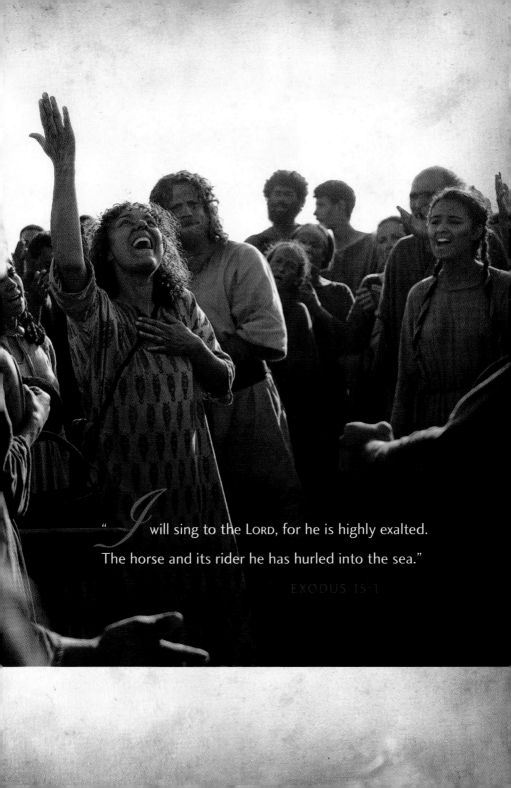

"*I* will sing to the Lord, for he is highly exalted.

The horse and its rider he has hurled into the sea."

EXODUS 15:1

"As it was in the days of Noah,

so it will be . . ."

MATTHEW 24:37

*O*ur series begins with creation. We tell this story through Noah and his family in the Ark during the storm, the likes of which none of us have ever seen or would wish to experience at sea. Noah tells his family the creation story as a means of keeping them calm and hopeful.

Today's text has Jesus telling his friends that he was going to come a second time. His first coming fulfilled hundreds of Old Testament prophecies of the coming of the Messiah as a "Suffering Servant." There are about the same number of unfulfilled prophecies of the return of Messiah as a "Conquering King."

The implication of what Jesus said in this passage is that a time is coming when the conditions that led to the Flood of Genesis will again exist in the modern world. The word that comes to mind when I think of Noah's world is *unsalvageable*. The author of Genesis notes that the wickedness on Earth had reached the place where the inclination of the hearts of humanity was "only evil continually." When conditions reached this level of dysfunction, God decided to start over.

With the spiritual state of the world in our time, and predictions such as the end of the Mayan calendar cycle pointing to the Apocalypse, what should our response be to this kind of thinking? First, the original Ark was what scholars call a "type." It symbolically pointed to the ultimate "Ark"—Jesus. We don't need a boat; we need a Savior! Once we have our "ticket" on Ark Jesus, we should have a radically different take on our world. Rather than despair about all that is wrong, I think Jesus continues to call us to turn up the "volume" on doing things that advance his kingdom. And the promise of Jesus, that he will be with us as we do, hasn't changed.

How about putting an "A" for "Ark" on your hand today, and do something to make a difference for the kingdom. *JM*

Father, please use me to shine your light.
Show me the way. Amen.

For he will command his angels concerning you to guard you in all your ways.

PSALM 91:11

Because of my years on *Touched by an Angel,* I love and believe in angels. I am strengthened and encouraged to imagine them with me. This passage reminds me that God himself has commanded them to be with us. These words fill us with respect for the presence of angels, inspire devotion because of their loving service, and instill confidence because of their protection.

The angels are here at our sides to protect us and guide us. Our loving Father has given them this charge, and we are grateful to the angels for the great love with which they obey God's command and come to help us in our time of need.

God in heaven, my Savior dear,
watch over me please and draw thou near.
Send your angels to be at my side,
to light and to guard, to love and to guide. R

Dear Father, we are so grateful that you have sent us your angels to guide us and protect us. We are grateful to have your loving angels at our sides. In Jesus' name we pray. Amen.

"I am the vine; you are the branches.
If a man remains in me and I in him,
he will bear much fruit."

JOHN 15:5

We live in Southern California. Several hours north of us lies the wine country of the Napa and Sonoma valleys. Whenever I read today's verse, it reminds me of the beauty of the vineyards that cover that part of the country.

Jesus is the master of metaphor, and today's verse contains one of my favorites. Jesus tells the disciples that he is the vine and they are branches of the vine. The words stir images of mature grapevines with large trunks spawning branches filled with ripe grapes. One day those grapes will be the source of fine wine. As long as the branch is connected to the vine, it thrives and bears fruit. But if the branch is somehow severed from the vine, it withers and dies.

God wants our lives to be productive. The Bible even uses the word *fruit* to describe spiritual productivity. The point of the vine and branch metaphor is to teach us that as we cultivate our relationship with Jesus, his life can flow through us, and we can be like those branches filled with grapes. But the fruit that Jesus produces in and through us is love, joy, peace, patience, kindness, gentleness, faithfulness, and self-control. The Bible even calls these qualities "the fruit of the Spirit."

In order for our lives to be spiritually productive, we need to stay vitally connected to Jesus. We are as dependent on his Spirit working in and through us as the branch is dependent upon the vine. When we get disconnected from Christ, we wither and die spiritually. When we stay connected, he is able to produce good results through our lives. The "wine" produced is the transformation of our own lives and the impact we have on the lives of others for Jesus and his kingdom.

Lord Jesus, help us abide in you today. Help us allow you to live in and through us. Bear good spiritual fruit through us. Keep us connected to you. In your name we ask. Amen.

When the LORD finished speaking to Moses on Mount Sinai, he gave him the two tablets of the Testimony, the tablets of stone inscribed by the finger of God.

EXODUS 31:18

"THEREFORE, I TELL YOU, HER MANY SINS

have been forgiven—for she loved much.

BUT HE WHO HAS BEEN FORGIVEN LITTLE

loves little."

LUKE 7:47

Jesus loves people. In *The Bible,* we show how he always seemed to be attracted to the underdog. He also had a special place in his heart for women. Today's verse is found in an incident that reflects how he treated the marginalized.

Jesus was having dinner at the home of a Pharisee named Simon. During dinner, a woman crashed the party. The description given in the Bible indicates that she was of questionable reputation. Later tradition identifies the woman as Mary Magdalene.

Imagine the scene. The woman enters weeping and carrying an alabaster jar of costly ointment. She falls at Jesus' feet and begins washing them with her tears and drying them with her hair. She pours out the costly oil on his feet. Meanwhile, Simon has a look on his face that tells all. He is wondering how Jesus could possibly be a prophet if he let a woman like this do what she was doing.

Jesus knows what Simon is thinking. He responds by telling a story about two men whose debts were forgiven. One owed two days' wages; the other, two years' wages. When asked which would have been more grateful, Simon answered, "The one who was forgiven more." After comparing how Simon treated him to how the woman treated him, Jesus gets to the point. This woman recognized how much she was forgiven and responded with out-rageous love. Simon had no clue.

We have been forgiven much. Jesus went to the cross to make that happen. When we come to grips with these realities, it should generate immense love in our hearts. This woman will probably still put us to shame, but she is the model . . . not Simon! 〰 *M*

Lord Jesus, you have forgiven us much, and it cost you greatly to do so. I hope that when we see you face-to-face, we will be able to understand the degree of love that was poured out on Calvary. Help us love you more. In your name we pray. Amen.

> "So may all your enemies perish, O LORD! But may they who love you be like the sun when it rises in its strength."
>
> JUDGES 5:31

A woman who led the people of Israel during the period of the Judges spoke today's verse. Her name was Deborah. In a patriarchal society, such as ancient Israel, Deborah must have been a very special woman to hold this position! She has been an inspiration to women throughout the centuries who have been called by God to positions of leadership.

The story from which this verse is taken involves a great battle between the armies of Israel and the Canaanite army of King Jabin. When the two armies engaged in the critical battle of the campaign, Deborah and the army of Israel put the Canaanites to flight. The commander of the Canaanite army, Sisera, took refuge in a tent, where another woman, named Jael, pounded a tent peg through his temple while he slept! The battle was over, and Deborah and the army of Israel were victorious. Israel enjoyed peace under Deborah's leadership for the next forty years. Today's text is the final line in the song Deborah wrote to celebrate the victory.

We will all probably fight a few battles today. Hopefully, we won't use the "tent peg through the temple" strategy to win them. But today's verse says that those who love God will have the advantage in the fight. It is a great image—you and I will "be like the sun when it rises in its strength." When we love God, he does not always take away the battles. We still face strong enemies as Deborah did. But he is with us in the midst of the battle to fight for us and with us.

Father, thank you that in the midst of the battles of life, you are with us. Thank you for the example of Deborah, a woman who loved you. Help us love you and experience your love in our lives. When we face the battles that this day holds, grant us the awareness that you are with us. Amen.

Delight yourself in the LORD . . .

PSALM 37:4

What is the desire of your heart? Today's text is followed by a great promise. It tells us that the outcome of following David's advice is that God "will give you the desires of your heart." I'm quite sure that this is not a reference to getting an expensive car. If a Mercedes Benz is the desire of your heart, your heart probably needs to change.

That is the beauty of today's text. When our focus shifts from earthly desire to heavenly desire, our hearts change. We begin to desire the things of God's kingdom. When the things of God's kingdom become our heart's desire, God will act. "Delight" and "desire" work hand in hand.

One way to apply this principle is to spend some time reading the Gospels. If you use your imagination to enter into the adventures of Jesus, you might find yourself growing and changing. You might experience a shift in perspective and find yourself desiring to experience more of God in your life. When our desires change, God will draw us closer to himself. As he draws us closer to himself, we will experience the fulfillment of our desire.

In episodes 6 through 8 of our series, we showed this adventure as Jesus gathered his disciples and began his ministry. In the feeding of the 5,000 scene, Jesus says, "Put God first and everything else will follow." This is true, and if you do this starting today, everything will immediately improve. Trust in God, breathe, believe, and perceive. *R*

Heavenly Father, we put our trust in you.
Loving you has changed our lives and
enriched our souls. We are grateful.
We put you first. We love you, and
we are grateful for all the blessings
you bestow on us. Amen.

*D*avid said to the Philistine,

". . . I come against you in the name of the L<small>ORD</small>

Almighty, the God of the armies of Israel,

whom you have defied."

1 SAMUEL 17:45

God blessed them and said to them,

"Be fruitful and increase in number;

fill the earth and subdue it.

Rule over the fish of the sea and the

birds of the air and over every living

creature that moves on the ground."

GENESIS 1:28

he first recorded action taken by God in relationship to the man and woman he had created was to bless them. It makes me think that one of the main reasons we were created was so that God could bless us. If that is so, part of the purpose for our lives is to experience the blessing of God.

Mark and I are blessed. We have each other. We have three beautiful children. We have had success in our careers. We have both come to a place in our lives where we know that God loves us. We also know that God's touch on our lives, on a daily basis, is what brings joy and purpose to our lives.

When we are in the right relationship with God and with one another, we experience a deep sense of well-being that takes place at the core of our being. It is a profound experience that takes place very deep inside. The Bible calls that place our spirit.

This experience is so important to us that we try to do those things that help us experience God's blessing and to avoid doing anything that would result in losing God's blessing.

We pray that you would experience God's blessing in your life. As you spend time reading these devotional thoughts, we pray you might sense God's touch on your life. God created you to bless you. Enjoy his blessing. ℳ ℛ

Heavenly Father, we need your touch on our lives.
We long to experience your love and your blessing.
It is the deepest need of our hearts. Bless us,
and help us be a source of blessing to all
we come in contact with today.
Amen.

There is no fear in love. But perfect love drives out fear . . .

1 JOHN 4:18

Many of us hold the hidden fear that God is angry with us. Somewhere in our youth or childhood, someone may have taught us that God had an angry voice and a paddle in his back pocket. And any time we go too far, we are afraid he is going to punish us and shame us. But the truth is, we have a Father who is full of love and compassion. And when we are hurting, we can turn to our Father because he cares for us.

We serve a God who is waiting to embrace us whether we succeed or fail. He loves us all because we are his children. When our hearts are open to his perfect love, there is no room for fear. In God's perfect love, we have come home. *R@M*

Dear God, we know we are at home in your love.
We know you love us with a perfect love.
You are our loving Father, and we are your children.
Thank you for your unconditional love.
Amen.

"But while he was still a long way off,
his father saw him and was filled with
compassion for him; he ran to his son,
threw his arms around him and kissed him."

LUKE 15:20

Jesus was a masterful storyteller. Today's verse comes from another of our favorite parables. It is usually called "The Parable of the Prodigal Son," but we think of it as "The Parable of the Loving Father." It is part of a trilogy of stories that Jesus told in the chapter from which today's verse is taken. After building the dramatic tension with the first two stories, Jesus launches into the tale of a wayward boy and the dad who loved him.

In the story, the son demands his share of his father's estate. He runs off to a faraway country and spends it all on wild living. The son ends up in a pigpen feeding pigs. Jesus said that when he came to his senses, he began to think about his father and the home he had abandoned. Feeling completely unworthy to even be called a son, and hoping his father would at least give him a job, he heads home.

We imagine the father going to the gate every day and looking down the road, hoping this is the day his son will return home. When he sees the boy in the distance, he runs to him and throws his arms around him and kisses him. He welcomes him home, overjoyed to see him, loving him unconditionally.

This is how our heavenly Father feels about us. Even when we stray from him and end up in the pigpen, he is longing for us to come home. The message of Jesus is plain: God's love is unconditional. Wherever you are in your spiritual life, he wants you to come home. He welcomes you with open arms. *RQM*

Heavenly Father, thank you for your unconditional love.
Thank you for giving us this beautiful story of
what your love is really like. Even when we feel
we have made too many mistakes for you to love us,
remind us that your love is different. You love us.
Amen.

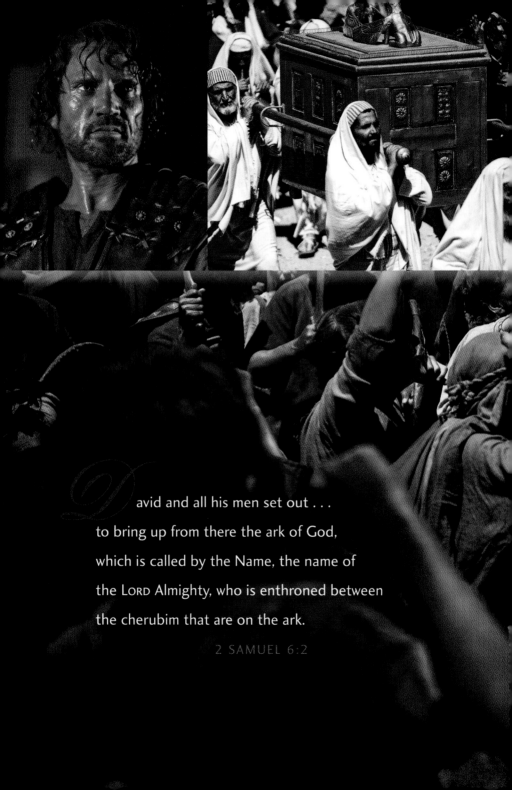

David and all his men set out . . .
to bring up from there the ark of God,
which is called by the Name, the name of
the Lord Almighty, who is enthroned between
the cherubim that are on the ark.

2 SAMUEL 6:2

"SO IN EVERYTHING,

do to others what you would

have them do to you,

FOR THIS SUMS UP THE LAW

and the Prophets."

MATTHEW 7:12

In *The Bible*, we show the genius of the things Jesus said and did. He had a way of taking common concepts and putting his own twist on them. When he did, the result was always profound. For instance, the Jewish Law contained certain precepts that were intended to restrain retaliation. You are probably familiar with the expression: "an eye for an eye, and a tooth for a tooth." In its original context, this law was designed to keep someone who lost an eye from retaliating by poking out both of the offender's eyes, and then knocking out all his teeth.

In the same way, under the Law, people were instructed not to do anything to another person they would not want that person to do to them. It was all about restraint. This law is now referred to as "The Silver Rule." The original is called silver because Jesus' variation of it created gold! Instead of a negative law about retaliation, Jesus created an approach to life that is proactive and positive. How do you want to be treated? Do you want people to be kind and loving toward you? Then that is how you are to treat others. When you have a "Golden Rule," you don't really need a "Silver Rule."

Jesus said that part of the greatest commandment was to love your neighbor as yourself. How do you do that? Do to them what you would like them to do to you! The Golden Rule brought heaven to earth. Imagine what the world would be like if everyone followed this one simple teaching of Jesus!

Lord Jesus, help me treat people the way you treat people.
Remind me to do to others the things I hope they would do to me.
I ask you to enable me to be kind and loving to the people you
bring into my life today. In your name I pray.
Amen.

"In the last days,
God says,
I will pour out
my Spirit
on all people.
Your sons and
daughters will
prophesy,
your young men
will see visions,
your old men
will dream
dreams."

ACTS 2:17

Part of what we hoped to accomplish by creating *The Bible* series was to show that the Bible is not simply a series of unconnected stories. We wanted to show how the Old Testament was connected to the New Testament, that it is one sweeping story of God and all of us. Today's verse comes from the story of Pentecost, when the Holy Spirit came in power and inspired the lives of the disciples. We filmed this scene in episode 10.

In today's verse, Peter is explaining to the crowd what was happening. He tells them, "This is what was spoken by the prophet Joel." He then quotes the book of Joel. An Old Testament prophecy about the coming of Messiah was being fulfilled. The Bible is filled with these kinds of connections. God was working out the plan that started with creation.

We can hardly imagine how thrilling the Pentecost experience must have been. The disciples were experiencing exactly what Jesus promised would happen, and they were experiencing the fulfillment of what God's prophets had been saying for hundreds of years. What we call the New Testament was fulfilling a prophecy from the Old Testament. It all ties together.

Creating *The Bible* series has given us a new appreciation for the Bible. We see clearly how it is all one grand story, a great sweeping love story. Our hope is that you will discover what we have discovered. God has given us a gift of inestimable value in the Bible. We try to read it daily, and the more time we read it, the closer we feel to God. ✍ *R&M*

Father, thank you for the gift of the Bible. It is such an amazing book. I know we often take it for granted. Help us realize how important it is in developing our relationship with you. Help us develop a habit of spending time in your Word. Amen.

"I will make you into a great nation and I will bless you; I will make your name great, and you will be a blessing. I will bless those who bless you, and whoever curses you I will curse; and all peoples on earth will be blessed through you."

GENESIS 12:2-3

The art of screenwriting includes a concept called "the inciting incident." This is the moment that launches the main story line and to which all of the rest of the story is connected. Today's verses could be called the "inciting incident" of the Bible. They record a promise God made to a man named Abraham. He is one of the central characters in Judaism, Christianity, and Islam.

Abraham grew up in the pagan culture of the ancient city of Ur. In the verses previous to today's verses, we read that God had called Abraham out of this center of civilization and told him to head toward a place that God would show him. He said that if Abraham would respond to this call, God would bless him. Abraham heard God's call and obeyed, then God blessed Abraham.

God blesses people. Blessing involves the experience of God touching us at the core of our being. It is a touch that brings healing and wholeness and is one of the deepest needs of the human heart. God created us to be blessed. When we don't experience God's blessing, we have a sense that something is missing in our lives. We feel an emptiness, a hunger inside.

God wants to bless you today. Throughout the day, hear him saying to you what he said to Abraham: *I will bless you.* God's love will fill the emptiness. May you be blessed. *R*

Heavenly Father, we desperately need your touch on our lives. Only you can meet the deepest needs and desires of our hearts. Bless us today. Help us become a source of blessing to all we meet. Amen.

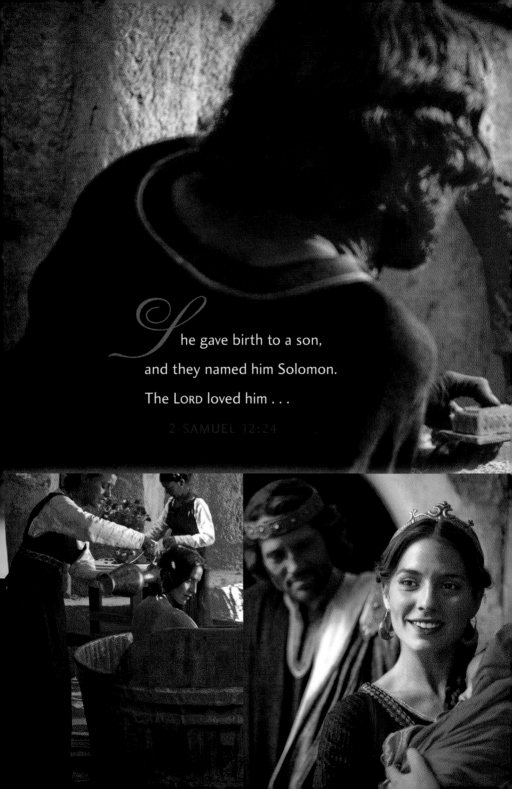

She gave birth to a son,
and they named him Solomon.
The LORD loved him . . .

2 SAMUEL 12:24

I know whom I have believed,
and am convinced that he is able
to guard what I have entrusted
to him until that day.

2 TIMOTHY 1:12

You have heard the old saying, "It's not what you know, but who you know that counts." Never is that more true than when it comes to the spiritual life. Authentic faith isn't nearly as much about what you know as it is about whom you believe in.

Today's verse is taken from some of the last words the apostle Paul wrote. A little later in the letter Paul tells Timothy that God has made known to him that the "time for my departure" (his death) was at hand. Shortly after writing Timothy, the great apostle was beheaded in Rome by the maniacal Roman Emperor Nero.

Few of us will face the magnitude of difficulty Paul experienced. Most of his friends had deserted him. He was facing death. And yet he had confidence in the midst of his trials. He knew in whom he had believed: Jesus. He knew that even in death, he was the victor.

Life can be difficult. Circumstances will not always turn out the way we would have scripted them. But in the midst of life's difficulties and challenges, God is there. Faith is a trust that knows that when we believe in Jesus and commit our lives to him, he will be with us in whatever life throws our way. In those times, we should remember these words of Paul: "I know whom I have believed, and am convinced he is able!"

If you are in a time of struggle, be encouraged. God loves you. He has not abandoned you. He cares. *RGM*

Father, sometimes we get discouraged by the struggles we face. But deep in our hearts, as was true of Paul, we know you can be trusted. Lord Jesus, thank you that in the end, we are yours, and you are able to help us get through life's difficulties. Thank you that you never leave us or forsake us. In your name we pray. Amen.

> To them God has chosen to make known among the Gentiles the glorious riches of this mystery, which is Christ in you, the hope of glory.
>
> COLOSSIANS 1:27

For many years of my life, God was more a matter of the head than of the heart. I knew facts about Jesus from the Bible, but I didn't know him personally. This was not the case with Roma. She began to know Jesus personally as a young girl, after the death of her mum. Her faith was such a source of comfort and strength to her and her family. My feelings about religion were quite different. I thought of religion as something that was always telling me that the things I was doing were wrong.

Today's verse was written by the apostle Paul. When we first see Paul in *The Bible,* he is a religious fundamentalist who knows all the rules but does not have a heart connection with God. All that changed for Paul on the road to Damascus when Jesus appeared to him. In an instant, Paul knew that his entire understanding of God was wrong. God didn't just want to be in Paul's head; he wanted to dwell in his heart. In today's verse, Paul says that the mystery of God is "Christ *in* you." It is this indwelling presence of Jesus that makes the spiritual connection God desires.

Everything changed for me when I slowly began to understand that God loved me. The idea of a relationship with him, instead of a lot of rules, began to sink in. I discovered that I could open my heart to God and invite him into my life. When I took that step, everything changed. Have you discovered this "mystery"? It will make all the difference in your life.

M

Father, we are so grateful that you are not looking for performance but relationship. Thank you that when we open our hearts and invite Jesus to come into our lives, he does. Amen.

*The disciples went and woke him, saying,
"Master, Master, we're going to drown!"
He got up and rebuked the wind and the raging
waters; the storm subsided, and all was calm.*

LUKE 8:24

We experienced some challenging times as we filmed the scenes in *The Bible* that took place with Jesus and the disciples on the Sea of Galilee. Just like in today's verse, "the winds came up on the lake." Our crews struggled to keep equipment from blowing away, and we all hoped none of the disciples were going to be blown out of the boat and into the water!

We can only imagine that Jesus must have been exhausted when the event recorded in these verses took place. He had just healed a multitude of people and exorcized a great many demons. He was sleeping through the storm, until the disciples woke him. To demonstrate that he had power over the forces of nature, he calmed the storm by commanding the wind and waves to be still.

There are some days when our lives feel like we are in a boat, in the middle of the ocean, with the winds blowing and the waves crashing around us. In these times, God wants us to know he can calm the storm. He also wants us to know that when he chooses not to calm the storm, he can calm us.

We don't know what storm you are facing today. You might feel overwhelmed by a storm in your finances. Maybe you have a storm in your marriage or family. Maybe your storm involves your health. Whatever you are facing, God cares. You can take your problems to him. Call out to the Lord today, and we believe he will either calm the storm or work in your heart to calm you and give you faith and hope and remind you that you are loved. *ROM*

Lord Jesus, you are the one who calms the storm.
You are concerned for our lives. You know everything
going on in our lives. We need your help today.
We ask you to either change our circumstances
or give us your peace. We thank you today
for all your love. Amen.

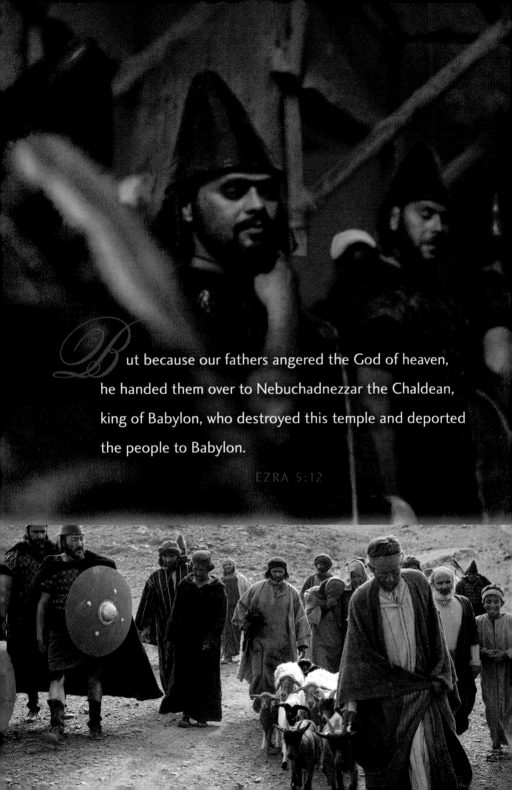

But because our fathers angered the God of heaven, he handed them over to Nebuchadnezzar the Chaldean, king of Babylon, who destroyed this temple and deported the people to Babylon.

EZRA 5:12

THE LORD CAME AND STOOD THERE,

calling as at the other times,

"Samuel! Samuel!"

THEN SAMUEL SAID, "SPEAK,

for your servant is listening."

1 SAMUEL 3:10

*I*n episode 3 of *The Bible* series, we first meet Samuel when he is an old man. Today's verse is from his childhood. Samuel's mother had dedicated him to the Lord as an act of gratitude for God healing her barrenness. She named him Samuel, a name that means "God hears," because God had heard her prayer. Providentially, Samuel would also be a man who heard God.

At the time God called Samuel, God's voice had not been heard for some time. The larger passage from which today's verse is taken includes the words, "the word of the Lord was rare." That was about to change. Samuel heard God, then he spoke what God said, and he became a great prophet.

Most of us will not hear God speak in the way Samuel did. We will probably not be prophets in the biblical sense of the word. But all of us can hear God speak to us in our own lives. Our relationship with God is designed to be dynamic, not static. A few rare individuals might get "audibles," as Samuel did, but most of us will hear the voice of God in a more internal way.

As we pray, we might have a sense that God is communicating with us. When we read the Bible in a thoughtful way, we might sense something in the text jump out at us. When we get away to a quiet place and simply sit in the presence of the Lord, we might sense an inner voice communicating. These are all ways that God speaks. The challenge is for us to learn to listen. Take some time today to read the Bible and pray. Ask God to speak to you. See if you "hear" his voice. *R@M*

Father, I want to hear you speaking to me.
Help me take the time to read your Word,
spend quiet time in prayer, and simply slow down and listen.
Teach me to hear your voice. Amen.

> Then Caleb silenced the people before Moses and said, "We should go up and take possession of the land, for we can certainly do it."
>
> NUMBERS 13:30

By nature, when someone tells me I can't do something, it motivates me to try. Roma is the same. We are adventurous, and we know what it means to take risks. Undertaking *The Bible* was a big adventure . . . and a big risk! In this way, we are a lot like Caleb and Joshua—two of the twelve spies sent into the Promised Land.

Today's verse takes place at the point in the Exodus of Israel when the tribes of Israel were camped in the desert and positioned to take possession of what God had promised. Twelve men, including Joshua and Caleb, were sent by Moses to reconnoiter the Promised Land.

When the spies returned from spying out the land, all twelve reported that it was a good land, flowing with milk and honey. But ten of the twelve did not have faith enough to be brave. They were not by nature as adventurous as Caleb and Joshua. They told the people that there were giants in the land, and that the Israelites could not defeat them.

This incident reminds me of what we often face in our lives as people of faith. We think God might be asking us to take a risk. We carefully analyze the situation and discover that there are "giants" in the land. What God asks is going to have big challenges. We faced this when we started talking about making *The Bible.* But we knew God was with us in the adventure.

We want you to know that God is bigger than the giants in your life. God wants you to succeed. But you need to listen to your faith and take risks, even though it feels scary. What is more scary is the idea of looking back on having not taken that risk and spending your life wandering in the wilderness as the Israelites ended up doing. He wants you to be like Caleb and say, "We can certainly do it!" *M*

Father, whatever challenges we face today, we are not alone. You are here. You lead us to a life of adventure and risk. Keep us from being foolish, but keep us from being afraid. Help us remember that with faith, "We can do it!" With you, all things are possible. We praise your name. Amen.

*"On that same night I will pass through Egypt
and strike down every firstborn . . .
The blood will be a sign for you on the houses
where you are; and when I see the blood,
I will pass over you."*

EXODUS 12:12–13

These were the words God spoke to Moses as he was about to free the children of Israel from slavery in Egypt. They are part of the event we call the Passover. God provided an escape from death and destruction through an act of faith, where the blood of a lamb would be applied to the doorposts of the homes of the Israelites. When the Angel of Death saw the blood, he would "pass over" that house. All inside would be safe.

After four hundred years of slavery, as the Lord had promised Abraham (Genesis 15:13), the time had come for the children of Israel to be freed from their bondage and led to the Promised Land. The seventy men and women of the family of Isaac had grown to an approximated three million. Filming these events for *The Bible* made us feel as though we were right there with Moses. They also reminded us of how the Passover was a picture of what Jesus would do when he became "the lamb of God who takes away the sins of the world." Those words of John the Baptist were a direct reference to the words of today's verses.

We want everyone to experience the love of God. Our hope and prayer in creating *The Bible* series was that many who do not have a relationship with God would rethink where they stand in their spiritual lives. Where are you today with God? Jesus died to make it possible to experience God's love. Open your heart to him today.

R&M

Father, thank you for sending Jesus
to be the true Lamb of God.
Thank you, Lord, for giving your life
so that we could have life.
Amen.

*N*ow when Daniel learned that the decree had
been published, he went home to his upstairs room
where the windows opened toward Jerusalem.
Three times a day he . . . prayed, giving thanks
to his God, just as he had done before.

DANIEL 6:10

DAY 45

For the word of God

is living and active. Sharper than any

double-edged sword, it penetrates

even to dividing soul and spirit,

joints and marrow; it judges the thoughts

and attitudes of the heart.

HEBREWS 4:12

The Bible is unlike any other book in the world. Today's verse calls it "the word of God." *The Bible* series attempts to capture this magnificent book in visual form.

Many books are written to either entertain or inform you. The Bible will do both. But reading, studying, memorizing, and meditating on this book will change your life! Today's verse is set in a context where the writer describes living in dynamic relationship with God. He writes about living so in the center of God's will that our lives are characterized by serenity, peacefulness, and a lack of striving to earn God's favor. In the larger passage, this is called God's "rest."

The Bible, when used by the Spirit of God, has the ability to influence us at the depths of our inner being. The writer of Hebrews expresses this by saying it penetrates as deep as the division between the soul and spirit, joints and marrow. The Bible's influence goes all the way to the heart of our thoughts and attitudes. When we read in the right spirit, with an openness to God's work through us, this is a book that can change our lives.

We try to spend time reading the Bible every day. It can help to use a journal and write out what you sense God is trying to say to you. Often, as you engage the Bible in this way, you will feel God's presence. Parts of the text will jump out at you, almost as if God is saying, "Here it is!" If you don't have a habit of daily encounter with the Bible, begin the practice today. It will change your life! *ℛ*

Father, thank you for the gift of the Bible.
Thank you that it is your Word. Thank you that
through it you communicate with us.
Thank you that you use it to change our lives.
Help us to spend time with you today.
We want to spend time reading the Bible every day.
We are inspired by your Word. Amen.

> Hear, O Israel: The LORD our God, the LORD is one. Love the LORD your God with all your heart and with all your soul and with all your strength.
>
> DEUTERONOMY 6:4–5

The main purpose of life is to love God and to love other people. It was the reason we created *The Bible* series.

There is a moment in *The Bible* where the people of Israel arrive at the east bank of the Jordan River, finally positioned to take possession of the land God had promised to Abraham, some four hundred years earlier. Leadership was about to pass from Moses to Joshua. Exactly at this moment, Moses delivered a message that is found in our Bibles under the title *Deuteronomy*. Today's verses are from that speech.

When Moses said, "Hear, O Israel: the LORD our God, the LORD is one," he reminded the people of who brought them out of slavery and who was going to take them into the land: God. The God.

The words of Moses contain the logical response to this truth. If God is God, we should "love the LORD your God with all your heart and with all your soul and with all your strength." When asked about the greatest commandment, Jesus quoted this passage. He went on to add, "Love your neighbor as yourself" (Matthew 22:39). Jesus said these two commands summarized all God wanted to teach through the Law and all the Prophets.

Jesus wants us all to know that the purpose of life is to love God and love one another. We are trying to make this the main purpose of our lives. We invite you to join us. *M*

Heavenly Father, we acknowledge today that you are God. We desire to love you and grow in that love. As we learn to love you, teach us also to love one another the way we should. Amen.

The words of the Teacher, son of David,
king in Jerusalem: "Meaningless! Meaningless!"
says the Teacher. "Utterly meaningless!
Everything is meaningless."

ECCLESIASTES 1:1–2

Solomon was a complex person. He was the son of King David and inherited the throne of the kingdom of Israel at the height of its glory. He asked God for wisdom and received more wisdom than any man before him and every man that followed, until the coming of Jesus Christ. He was the richest man in the world. He had everything "the good life" had to offer. And yet, at the time when he wrote today's verses, he was experiencing complete disillusionment with life. He was the first modern man. He achieved everything he set out to accomplish and came up empty!

The King James Version of today's text reads, "Vanity, vanity . . . all is vanity." Our version captures the more accurate sense of emptiness and lack of meaning Solomon was experiencing: "Meaningless! Everything is meaningless." Ecclesiastes could have been written yesterday. It reflects many of the same quests modern men and women spend their lives pursuing. It sends a message that too few understand in time. Life is not about power, possessions, prestige, or popularity. These things will never meet the deep needs of our lives. We all hunger for meaning. We all hunger for God.

The purpose of life is to love God and one another and to live life with the values and principles God has revealed in the Bible. With God in our hearts, our lives feel full with purpose and meaning. We are grateful. *RGM*

Father, help us today to live in a way that
does not lead to emptiness and despair.
Help us know that many of the things we
are told will make us happy will not accomplish
that goal. Keep us in the kind of relationship with
you that brings peace, purpose, and fulfillment.
Amen.

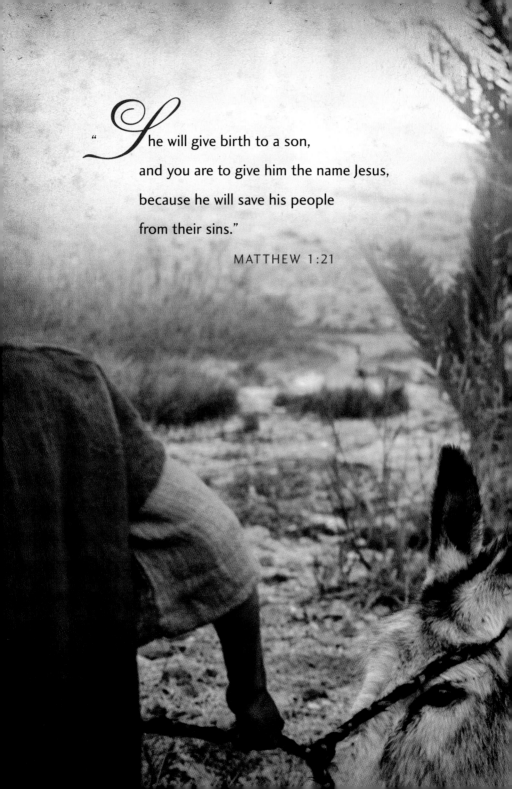

"She will give birth to a son,
and you are to give him the name Jesus,
because he will save his people
from their sins."

MATTHEW 1:21

THIS IS WHAT THE WICKED ARE LIKE—

always carefree,

they increase in wealth.

SURELY IN VAIN I HAVE KEPT MY HEART PURE;

in vain have I washed

my hands in innocence.

PSALM 73:12–13

One of the great spiritual questions many people wrestle with is the issue of why good people sometimes suffer, while so many bad people prosper. It is not a new question. Our verses today are from a psalm written by a man named Asaph. He was one of King David's chief musicians, who wrote this psalm after struggling with this very issue!

Earlier in the psalm, Asaph tells us that he found himself envying the prosperity of those he identifies as "the wicked." As he looks at what appears to be the lack of fairness in the world, he becomes discouraged about trying to live a righteous life.

His conclusion about those who thumb their noses at God is that "the evil conceits of their minds know no limits." And yet, he observes, "always carefree, they increase in wealth." Consequently, he reaches the conclusion of today's text: "Surely in vain I have kept my heart pure."

What does Asaph do to get his head back on straight? He steps back and looks at the "bigger" picture. He goes to "church." There he remembers some of the good things that we can't see in the visible world: God is always with us. God guides us and gives us strength. When our life ends, God takes us into his presence. As a result of getting his perspective straight, Asaph can say to God, "In this life, I don't need anything more than to be with you!"

When you try to live in a way that is pleasing to God, it is not in vain. If it seems as though the "bad guys" are always winning, remember that we have a very limited perspective. As did Asaph, we need to get ourselves into a place where we can get some perspective. It can change our discouragement to joy! We can go from victims to victors! *M*

Heavenly Father, help us remember that living
in a way that pleases you is never in vain.
Help us have your perspective on life. Thank you
for always being with us and for loving us. Amen.

And the scripture was fulfilled that says, "Abraham believed God, and it was credited to him as righteousness," and he was called God's friend.

JAMES 2:23

What a wonderful thought for today—to consider yourself a friend of God. If you have faith in God today, then just like Abraham, you are God's friend. And the Bible says that God is a friend who sticks closer than a brother. You can go to him anytime for anything. He will never leave you or forsake you. He will listen as you pour your heart out to him, and his ears never grow weary. We have his utmost and undivided attention.

So never forget that the Lord is your friend and that, as is true of friends, he wants to hear from you. He wants to know what has been happening in your life, good or bad, whether it is sorrowful or angry or joyful. God is there for you, through it all. You can count on him. *R*

Dear God, we turn to you in prayer and thank you for being such a wonderful friend. We can tell you anything, and we know you will understand and always be there for us. We know you will never let us down, Jesus, and for this we are truly grateful. Amen.

*"The thief comes only to steal and kill and destroy;
I have come that they may have life,
and have it to the full. I am the good shepherd.
The good shepherd lays down his life for the sheep."*

JOHN 10:10–11

I fell in love with Jesus when I was a little girl. I was only ten years of age when my mother died. It was the most influential tragedy of my life. She was just a young woman when she died of a heart attack, and I was especially close to her. I felt as if the lights of my life had been turned out when she dropped dead. My childhood experience went from coming home to a brightly lit happy home, with a fire in the fireplace, to one of emptiness and loneliness. The empty fireplace, without a fire, was a cold reminder of our loss.

But it was in that loneliness and emptiness that I found Jesus— or I should say that he found me. In the sadness and quietness of those days, he was there. I felt his presence. He was the warmth. His love was like a fire in the hearth. Today's verses say it in such a poetic way. He is the Good Shepherd. He was my Shepherd in those days when I was a lost little lamb. He is my Shepherd today, as I experience his love and care on a daily basis.

I love to remind people that God loves them. During my time on *Touched by an Angel*, I took the days when we shot Monica speaking those words very seriously. It was my prayer that those who were watching would know that the words were true, and that the audience at home would be touched by the message. Mark and I have prayed that the same message of God's love permeates *The Bible* series.

God loves you today. He wants you to know and experience that he is your Good Shepherd. He has come to give you life and to give it in abundance. I pray that you can sense his presence today and experience his love. *R*

Lord Jesus, thank you that you are
our Good Shepherd. Thank you that
you came to give us a more abundant life.
We pray that we would experience you today
and your love for us. Amen.

*T*he next day John saw Jesus coming toward him and said, "Look, the Lamb of God, who takes away the sin of the world!"

JOHN 1:29

"Then say to him, 'The LORD,

the God of the Hebrews, has sent me

to say to you: Let my people go,

so that they may worship me in the desert.

But until now you have not listened.'"

EXODUS 7:16

The Bible is filled with many men and women who are heroes of our faith. Moses was one of the greatest. Today's verse contains the iconic words God told Moses to speak to Pharaoh: "Let my people go!"

The children of Israel had spent four centuries in slavery. The time had come for them to be freed from bondage and led to the Promised Land. The parting of the Red Sea is one of the most cinematic moments in the entire Bible series (episode 2).

The story of the Exodus is a great metaphor for all of our lives. The Exodus serves as a picture of coming out of slavery into the Promised Land—into the life he has promised for all of us. And, of course, wandering in the wilderness would represent those times when we stray from God and lose our sense of his presence in our lives.

It can be helpful to use these images in our series to take inventory of where we are with God. Are we wandering in the wilderness, needing to get back to God, or are we enjoying God in the Promised Land? We are working to spend as much time in the "Promised Land" as possible. *R&M*

Father, thank you that through Jesus
we can be free to experience your love for us.
Help me to experience that love and spend as
much time enjoying you as possible.
You have promised us eternal hope,
and we are so grateful to you.
In your name we pray. Amen.

> If we confess
> our sins,
> he is faithful
> and just
> and will forgive
> us our sins
> and purify us
> from all
> unrighteousness.
>
> 1 JOHN 1:9

We recently had a company come to vacuum out the heating/air conditioning duct system that runs unseen throughout our entire house. They arrived with a vacuum so large it barely fit in the back of a semitruck. Over time, even with the best of housecleaning, dirt builds up in the duct system, resulting in a fine layer of dust throughout the house. Their job was "to go where no man has gone before"—into the belly of the beast, as it were.

After they left, we were thinking about how this experience was a good metaphor for what we periodically could use in our spiritual lives: a deep cleansing of the parts that no one sees but God. Even when we take care of the surface "dust" in our lives, deep down there can be something that keeps us from true spiritual purity. The "dust" is a reminder that something much deeper needs to be addressed.

Today's verse tells us that God is in the cleaning business. We know we aren't perfect. When we let him, the Holy Spirit will go to work in the deep places of our lives. John tells us that if we get honest with God and confess our sins, he will not only forgive us but will "cleanse" or "purify" us from all unrighteousness. When we confess, he "vacuums." Take some time today and let the Holy Spirit do some work in you! *RGM*

Heavenly Father, thank you that in your love for us you desire truth in the innermost places of our being. Thank you for the work of the Holy Spirit in those deep places. Reveal to us today any area of our life we need to allow you to work in. We desire to experience your forgiveness and cleansing today. Amen.

"Enter through the narrow gate. For wide is
the gate and broad is the road that leads to
destruction, and many enter through it.
But small is the gate and narrow the road that
leads to life, and only a few find it."

MATTHEW 7:13–14

Jesus spoke the words of today's verses on a small hill overlooking the beautiful Sea of Galilee. They are part of what has come to be known as "The Sermon on the Mount." In today's verses, Jesus paints a picture of two radically different paths in life. Not unlike Robert Frost's "The Road Not Taken," Jesus speaks of tough choices that need to be made to walk the path that leads to true life.

Roads represent ways of living. There is a way of life that at first glance may seem to be the easy road. The crowds take it. It is marketed by popular culture as the way to be happy. It is a road that is strewn with the wreckage of the lives of people who made the easy choice, followed the crowd, and ended up with a life filled with futility.

The other is the road less traveled. Those who are willing to pay the price and follow the narrow path of the Spirit travel it. But it is a rewarding path. It is the road to fulfillment through him.

You might be at a crossroads in your life. You might be facing choices that will determine the outcome of your life. Good choices will produce blessings and help you find a way to experience God's love and a life of meaning and fulfillment. *R*

Lord Jesus, you are the way, the truth, and the life.
We need you to help us make the choices
that put us on the loving path. We want
the meaning and purpose only you can give.
Help us make the right choices today.
In your name we pray. Amen.

"And I tell you that you are Peter, and on this rock I will build my church, and the gates of Hades will not overcome it."

MATTHEW 16:18

THE KING WAS OVERJOYED AND GAVE

orders to lift Daniel out of the den.

AND WHEN DANIEL WAS LIFTED FROM THE DEN,

no wound was found on him,

because he had trusted in his God.

DANIEL 6:23

One of the most dramatic scenes in *The Bible* series is when Daniel is thrown into the lions' den (episode 5). The king has given an order that anyone who prays will be punished by death. Daniel has been asked to choose between the order of an earthly king or faithfulness to the Lord God. He chooses God and makes a choice to pray. As a result, Daniel is fed to the lions.

Daniel had the faith and belief that God will deliver him, and God does. Daniel decided not to be a victim but to be victorious. Through his faith in God, Daniel receives victory. So much so that thousands of years later, this is one of the most iconic stories of the Bible. Daniel's faith is still inspiring us today.

When we believe and have faith, we understand that with God in our lives, we cannot fail. "For he is the living God and he endures forever; his kingdom will not be destroyed, his dominion will never end. He rescues and he saves; he performs signs and wonders in the heavens and on the earth. He has rescued Daniel from the power of the lions" (Daniel 6:26–27). For with God, all is possible! ✐ *R&M*

Dear God, we draw strength
from your endless love and live in your
limitless grace. Protect us today and every day.
We choose to love you above all.
Amen.

> "You intended to harm me, but God intended it for good to accomplish what is now being done, the saving of many lives."
>
> GENESIS 50:20

Life is sometimes not fair. Jesus warned his disciples that in this world they would have trouble (John 16:33). A relationship with God does not eliminate problems; rather, it gives us hope and perspective in the midst of whatever life throws our way. This is the message of the life of Joseph. Today's verse comes from his story.

Joseph was the son of Jacob, grandson of Isaac, and great-grandson of Abraham. His life was marked by repeated instances of unfairness. His brothers beat him and sold him into slavery in Egypt; he was falsely accused of sexual assault by his boss's wife and ended up in prison; promises made by fellow inmates were forgotten, resulting in him staying in prison longer than he should have. But God was at work in all of this.

Through the many twists and turns, Joseph slowly moved up the ranks of Pharaoh's servants. He ultimately became the most powerful man in Egypt, next to Pharaoh. God had a plan that was able to take the unfairness the fallen world had dished out to Joseph and use it for bigger purposes.

When payback time came with his brothers, Joseph took the high road. He had seen God work in his own life. He had an understanding that whatever was happening in the world, no matter how bad it might look, was probably part of the bigger plans of God. He was able to say to his brothers, "You intended to harm me, but God intended it for good."

God is at work in your life today. Whatever your circumstance, trust that God is at work in your life. Have faith in him. ✍ *M*

Father, help us trust you today. When we are treated unfairly or our lives feel unmanageable, help us remember that you are at work, and we can trust you. Amen.

"Be holy, because I am holy."

1 PETER 1:16

In The Bible series, we show Moses receiving the Law from God on Mt. Sinai (episode 2). It was at that time that God commanded the children of Israel to be holy, because he was holy. That message in the Old Testament is quoted in our verse for today.

Have you ever thought of yourself as holy? You may think that being holy is reserved for saints, priests, monks, and pastors—that only those people can be holy. But anyone can be holy. Holiness is an internal realization that only God's Spirit can produce in our lives. That is why he is called the *Holy* Spirit.

The word *holy* simply means that something is different or special. Specifically, it refers to common items such as loaves of bread and cups of wine that are set apart for sacred use. We are created to be holy. We are designed to be common people who get "set apart" to live in relationship with God. When we open our lives to Jesus, we immediately become holy in God's eyes. The act of surrender to God implies that we are giving ourselves to him. We are allowing him to use us for his purposes. We are "set apart" and "different." We might look exactly the same on the outside, and even act in many of the same ways we did before this transition, but inside everything is different. The common has become sacred. *R*

Heavenly Father, we don't think of ourselves as being very holy. But you tell us that is exactly what you want us to be. Thank you that true holiness is a matter of the heart. Only you can make us holy. Today, we give ourselves to you to be used for your purposes. Holy God, we praise your name. Amen.

"*B*lessed is the king who comes in the name of the Lord!"

LUKE 19:38

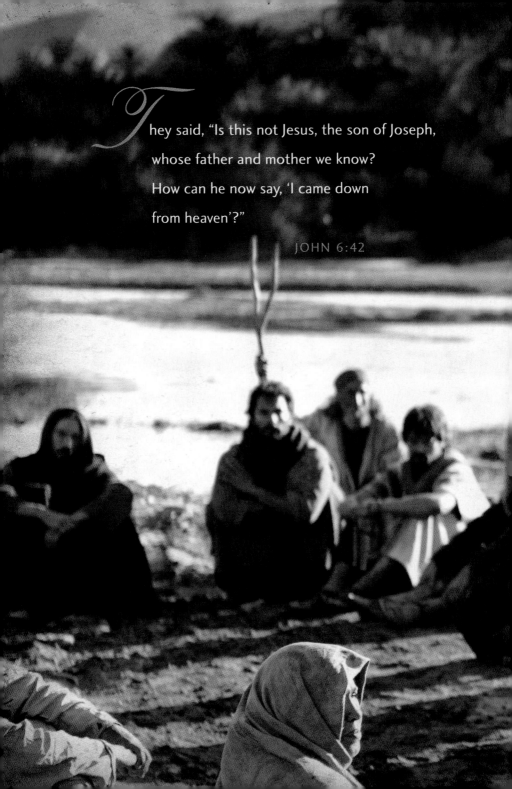

They said, "Is this not Jesus, the son of Joseph, whose father and mother we know? How can he now say, 'I came down from heaven'?"

JOHN 6:42

Then Manoah inquired of the angel

of the LORD, "What is your name,

so that we may honor you when

your word comes true?"

He replied, "Why do you ask my name?

It is beyond understanding."

JUDGES 13:17–18

oday's verse comes from one of the many incidents in the Bible where God sends an angel to deliver a message. The word *angel* actually means "messenger." This particular encounter took place when the angel of the Lord came to tell Manoah and his wife that they were going to have a son. His name was Samson, and he is a major character in *The Bible* series.

Samson's father asked the angel his name. The angel of the Lord told him that it was beyond Manoah's ability to comprehend. The truth is, we don't know everything there is to know about God.

If we study the Bible and read good books about our faith, we can learn an amazing amount of information about God. But the Bible periodically reminds us that God is bigger than our ability to completely understand him. In the realm of faith, there is always a degree of mystery. We live by faith, not by sight.

We know what God has made known to us about himself. But we don't know everything. In other words, God is bigger than our brains. Bigger than we can even imagine. Today, realize that all we know about God is only a tiny fraction of who he is. Marvel in the mystery!

Father, you have made yourself known to us.
You have told us that you loved the world so much
that you sent your Son, Jesus. You have come in the person
of your Holy Spirit to create life in our hearts where
there was once only death. We marvel today
at the mystery of who you are. Amen.

Moses said to God, "Suppose I go to the Israelites and say to them, 'The God of your fathers has sent me to you,' and they ask me, 'What is his name?' Then what shall I tell them?" God said to Moses, "I AM WHO I AM. This is what you are to say to the Israelites: 'I AM has sent me to you.'"

EXODUS 3:13–14

God has a name. It is not "God." That is his title. Moses was the first person whom God told. Today's verses record the incident. It took place during the experience Moses had when God appeared to him via the burning bush on Mt. Sinai. Moses asked who he should say was sending him back to Egypt. The answer he was given was that God's name is "I AM." "I AM" is the meaning of the Hebrew word YHWH, which is actually his name. God's name tells us three important facts about God.

God is the Creator. God is the one who causes everything that exists to exist. He has always existed, but in a moment in eternity, he created the universe. We are all part of his creation. We were in the mind of God before the universe came into existence. He cares about all of us.

God is sovereign. He is in control. His name reflects that he will be who he will be. He has plans and purposes for the entire universe, and he has plans and purposes for us. When the world seems out of control or our lives seem hopeless, remember that God is always in control. At the highest levels of ultimate reality, God controls all things. We can trust him.

God is eternal. He has always been, and he will always be. He is the God who is! He exists and will always exist. This all-powerful, all-knowing, all-loving, sovereign Creator loves all of us and wants us to experience his love today and every day. ✍ *RQM*

Father, you have made yourself known to Moses and many of the great men and women of faith throughout the ages. Thank you that you care for me. Help me experience your presence and love today.
Amen.

"But you will receive power when the Holy Spirit comes on you; and you will be my witnesses in Jerusalem, and in all Judea and Samaria, and to the ends of the earth."

ACTS 1:8

I am a car buff. I am fortunate to have a small collection that includes a couple of American muscle cars. Growing up in England, I admired these American cars because America was so "cool." I saw all these amazing cars on TV shows, with their powerful engines, power windows, and incredible speed. Now I have the thrill of heading up Pacific Coast Highway and feeling the exhilaration of stepping on the gas of one of these classic beauties and feeling that power kick in.

The Bible talks a lot about power. In today's verse, Jesus makes a promise that he is going to send the Holy Spirit, and the Spirit will infuse the disciples with power. The power Jesus promises is not like the power my cars possess. The power Jesus gives is the power that helps me be the kind of man God intends for me to be.

My muscle cars have one critical need to maximize their power: gas. Without gas, it makes no difference how much power the car is supposed to have. It won't run. The same is true in our spiritual lives. We need to be filled with the right kind of "gas" to experience God's power in our lives. For me that means I need to read and reflect on the Bible every day. It is like filling up my spiritual gas tank. When my tank is "empty," I lose the power!

I believe God wants to help you be the kind of person he created you to be. He wants you to be loving and kind today. He has plans for your life. He has power to help you discover and live an effective life. Put a "P" on your hand today to remind you to ask for God's power. *JM*

Father, thank you for the gift of the Holy Spirit. Thank you that you give us power to live for you. Empower my life today. Fill me with your Spirit. Amen.

*J*esus knew that the time had come for him to leave this world and go to the Father. Having loved his own who were in the world, he now showed them the full extent of his love.

JOHN 13:1

And he took bread, gave thanks and broke it, and gave it to them, saying, "This is my body given for you; do this in remembrance of me."

LUKE 22:19

Then the LORD answered Job out of the storm.

He said: "Who is this that darkens

my counsel with words without knowledge? . . .

WHERE WERE YOU WHEN I LAID

the earth's foundation?

Tell me, if you understand."

JOB 38:1–2, 4

There are times in life when we all would like to ask God the question, "Why?" Such was the case of a man named Job. His story is found in the Old Testament book that bears his name.

Job lost everything. His wealth, health, and family were all wiped out by disaster. He had no clue that at another level of reality, cosmic dynamics were at work. All he knew was that he had gone from a position of blessing and privilege to sitting on an ash heap, grieving the loss of his children. Job's eventual question was, "Why me, God?"

God's response to Job's question was a series of his own questions, beginning with today's verses. Job didn't really have the ability to comprehend either the question he has asked or the answer he hoped for! But he finally gets it. He eventually responds to God with the words, "I spoke of things I did not understand, things too wonderful for me to know." The answer to the question, "Why?" is sometimes, "I don't know." We can add to that, "But I trust God."

We know what it is like to be at a place in your life where you would like to know "Why?" There is nothing wrong with wanting to know the answer to that question. Sometimes God will show you the answer. Sometimes the answer is "not yet." We all have to learn to trust God. *ou R*

Father, in this crazy world, things happen
that we don't understand. We are grateful when you
help us answer the "Why?" question. Give us the ability
to remember that sometimes we won't know the answer.
In those times, give us grace to trust you. Amen.

> To the Jews who had believed him, Jesus said, "If you hold to my teaching, you are really my disciples. Then you will know the truth, and the truth will set you free."
>
> JOHN 8:31-32

Are you free? It is an important question. We might say that as Americans, we are free. But how about you personally? We can live in a free country and still not have freedom in our inner life. In today's verses, Jesus speaks about a different kind of freedom. It is a freedom of the heart. This kind of freedom is something that happens internally in our lives as Jesus becomes a part of who we are.

This inner freedom of the Spirit is related to how the Word of God is being integrated into our lives. Before Jesus talks about being free, he says, "If you hold to my teaching." Other versions translate the words as: "If you abide in my word." But how do we abide in Jesus' word or teaching?

Abiding requires that we have a regular time to read and think about who Jesus is and what he taught. The four gospels are a good place to start, for they contain the story of the life and teaching of Jesus. One hope we had in creating *The Bible* series was that it would stimulate people to read the Bible.

Sometimes it helps to memorize the words Jesus spoke. Then you can take a verse such as, "Then you will know the truth, and the truth will set you free," and meditate upon its meaning to your life.

Finally, abiding also implies that we integrate truth into our lives. The outcome of abiding and integrating the truth is inner freedom. *RⓍM*

Father, thank you for giving us the Bible.
Thank you for how the life and teaching of Jesus
have been preserved for us down through the centuries.
Help me learn to abide in your Word. Help me know the truth.
Set me free. In Jesus' name. Amen.

Remember this: Whoever sows sparingly will also reap sparingly, and whoever sows generously will also reap generously. Each man should give what he has decided in his heart to give, not reluctantly or under compulsion, for God loves a cheerful giver.

2 CORINTHIANS 9:6–7

Generosity is a lovely quality for a person to possess. It also is good for you. In today's verses the apostle Paul points out that it is the person who is generous who "reaps generously." Your "return on investment" when you are generous in your giving is both spiritual and often material. Jesus said that generosity was like light filling your inner being. He taught us that "it is more blessed to give than to receive."

When we give, God has ways of either directly blessing us or making the resources we have go even further. In *The Bible*, we show the children of Israel leaving Egypt for the Promised Land. We also show the people entering and possessing the Promised Land under the leadership of Joshua. In the narration of the series, we explain that it took forty years to finally accomplish this feat. The people of Israel wandered in the desert for forty years. What we don't show, or attempt to explain, is that the Bible says their shoes and clothing didn't wear out during those years (Deuteronomy 29:5). God can make a little go a long way!

When we decide to give and look for ways to bless others, we often see the return of an abundant harvest in our own lives. For the more we give, the more we get. We are doubly blessed. *RM*

Father, you bless generosity. Create a generous spirit in us. Help us not be reluctant givers, but cheerful, even hilarious, in our giving. Prompt us not only to give of our resources but also of ourselves. Amen.

He was despised and rejected by men,
a man of sorrows, and familiar with suffering.

ISAIAH 53:3

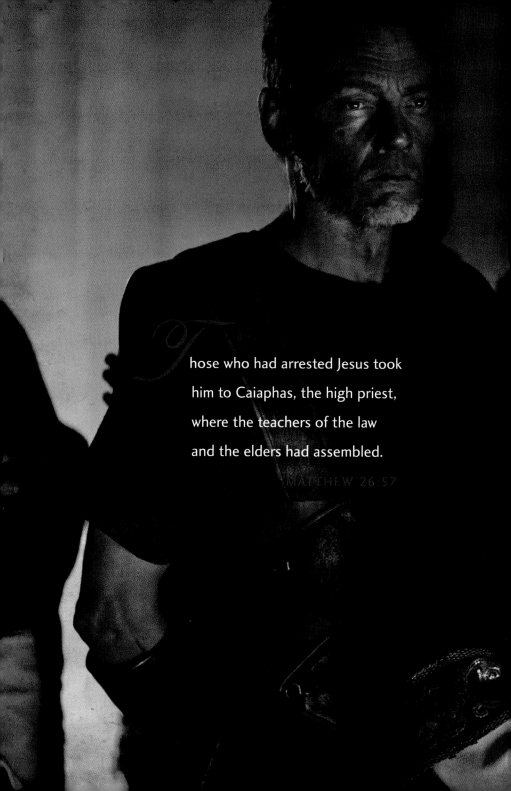

hose who had arrested Jesus took
him to Caiaphas, the high priest,
where the teachers of the law
and the elders had assembled.

MATTHEW 26:57

" *H*e is worthy of death."

MATTHEW 26:66

"Now fear the LORD and serve him

with all faithfulness. . . .

But if serving the LORD seems undesirable to you,

then choose for yourselves this day

whom you will serve, . . . But as for me

and my household,

we will serve the LORD."

JOSHUA 24:14–15

*J*oshua plays a major role in *The Bible* series. He leads the nation into the Promised Land after the death of Moses. We see him conquering Jericho in episode 3. Today's verses are classic, taken from the end of the fight to conquer the land of Canaan. Roughly forty years have passed since the battle of Jericho. The children of Israel were finally living in the land promised to Abraham.

With the passing of another generation, it was time to challenge the people again. Immediately before this verse, Joshua has rehearsed for the new generation all that God did to free them from slavery, protect them in the wilderness, and deliver their enemies into their hands. But a choice now needs to be made. It is a choice every man and woman faces in his or her life: "Who or what are you going to serve?"

Joshua challenged the people of Israel: "Choose for yourselves this day whom you will serve." Then he stated his own choice: "As for me and my household, we will serve the LORD!" The people responded that they also would serve God. They faithfully followed that choice for the rest of the years Joshua lived and beyond. Unfortunately, future generations would drift from the commitment made to Joshua on this day.

Who are we going to serve? In our world, the choices are seductive. Many choose to serve money. Others choose to serve fame. But for many, the answer is the one Joshua gave: "As for me and my household, we will serve the LORD."

Use this time today to ask yourself the question Joshua asked the children of Israel. If your answer is the same as Joshua's, tell God. You choose to serve him! *ROM*

Father, you have done so much for us that we
will serve you. Help us live out that decision today
and live in a way that pleases you.
We love you and choose to serve you!
It is an honor to do so. Amen.

> For the love
> of money
> is a root
> of all kinds
> of evil,
>
> 1 TIMOTHY 6:10

Today's text corrects a common misconception about what the Bible says about money. Many men and women think that the Bible teaches that money itself is the root of all evil. This would mean that there is something inherently bad about wealth itself, but that is not what the Bible teaches. It teaches that the *love* of money is a root, or source, of all kinds of evil.

There is a big difference. Wealth can be a good thing. It can be used to do wonderful things. It drives the economy and provides services, education, health, and rights for us all. It can also be a disastrous thing for some people. It ruins them. In today's text, the apostle Paul is writing to his young protégé, Timothy. He is warning Timothy to know when money has become a problem and what to do about it.

Paul counsels Timothy that contentment with godliness will protect him from the love of money that "plunges men into ruin and destruction." Strong language! The message of Jesus is to "love" people and "use" money. A little later in the passage, Paul tells Timothy to teach people to use their resources to "do good, be rich in good deeds, to be generous and willing to share."

We need to have that attitude toward prosperity—be successful, create wealth, and use our good fortune to spread goodness and prosperity. Love people and use money. *M*

Dear Father, open our hearts to loving you through our words and through our actions. May we be used to spread your Word. We pray in Jesus' name. Amen.

But when she could hide him no longer,
she got a papyrus basket for him
and coated it with tar and pitch.
Then she placed the child in it and put it
among the reeds along the bank of the Nile.

EXODUS 2:3

Pharaoh was culling the Hebrew population and killing all the baby boys. Moses' mother feared for her son's life. But instead of wallowing in fear, she stepped up and took action. With faith and courage and in spite of personal risk, she believed that God would protect her baby boy. She placed him in a basket on the River Nile—not knowing if he would drown or be eaten by crocodiles. But the one thing for sure was that if she kept him, he would be killed. He was placed on the river with a prayer to protect him, and that's exactly what God did, because he had a plan for Moses.

It is easy to become fearful when we can't see ahead. We are always hoping for certainty before we take action. We have to learn to set down our fears and worries, and then when our hands are free, we place our hands in God's hands.

When we face obstacles that seem insurmountable, we are reminded to have courage, to have faith, and to remember that God is with us.

When we boldly move ahead, it can release us from the bondage of fear. Worry and dread can take up free rent in our lives, but we need to remember that God is always with us. God is our strength. Our loving God will set us free. *R*

Loving Father, we know you are with us all day and every day. We ask that you remove any trace of fear or worry from our hearts and our minds and replace them instead with your strength and your love. Give us courage to move through our lives with courage and hope. Amen.

hen Simeon blessed them and said to Mary,

his mother: "This child is destined to cause

the falling and rising of many in Israel, and . . .

a sword will pierce your own soul too."

LUKE 2:34–35

SO GOD CREATED MAN

in his own image,

in the image of God he created him;

MALE AND FEMALE HE CREATED THEM.

GENESIS 1:27

Imago Dei. We love the sound of the phrase. It means "the image of God." The words tell us who we were created to be and express the value of every human life ever created. As we worked on *The Bible*, we found ourselves experiencing a new awareness and appreciation for the fact that we have been created in God's image.

In *The Bible*, Noah tells the story of creation as he and his family are tossed by the waves on the Ark. In episode 1, we have a beautiful scene as we actually show the creation of Adam and Eve. We also portray the temptation and fall of Adam and Eve. Because of the fall, the image of God in mankind has suffered distortion. But something of the image of God remains in every person.

Part of what happens when we open our hearts to God is the beginning of a process of transformation. God begins to change us from the inside out. His goal is to restore his image in us.

This is who we are. This is who every person you encounter today is. When you look in the faces of the people God brings along your path today, you are seeing people who were created in the image of God. It gives dignity and value to every human being. This truth should change the way you see yourself and the one whom Jesus calls your "neighbor." When you see God in everyone, you feel the loving connection to one another and to God. *R&M*

*Heavenly Father, thank you for creating us
in your image so that we can know you.
Help us experience your love today.
Help us remember that every person we meet
is infinitely valuable to you.
Help us treat them with your love. Amen.*

Then David said to Nathan,

"I have sinned

against the LORD."

2 SAMUEL 12:13

*E*pisode 4 of our series is where we tell this story of David. He is the second king of Israel, a hero who also behaves in a deplorable way. He sleeps with his friend's wife. It is one of the most notorious affairs in history. Even those who have never read the Bible have heard the story of David and Bathsheba. They might not get all the details right, but they get the general idea. But few know the outcome of the indiscretion.

David had been in the wrong place at the right time. He was supposed to be out on the battlefield where a king belongs when his army is at war. David is hanging out on the roof of the palace, and Bathsheba is taking a bath right in his line of sight. Taking advantage of his power as king, he brings her to the palace and commits adultery. Bathsheba gets pregnant from the one-night stand, and David tries to save face instead of getting honest with God. He brings Bathsheba's husband, Uriah, home from the battlefield and tries to get him to sleep with his wife, but it doesn't work. The heat is on. David then makes a horrible decision. As a cover-up for this affair and resulting pregnancy, he arranges for Uriah to be killed. He now is not only an adulterer; he is a murderer.

Fortunately for David, God has prophets. What might be hidden from the eyes of man is never hidden from the eyes of God. A prophet is some-one God uses to reveal what only God knows. Nathan had been placed in David's life for just such a time as this. I say "fortunately," because the worst thing that could have possibly happened to David would have been for him to get away with what he did. It would have eventually ruined him. God loved him enough to keep that from happening.

We would encourage you to read the entire chapter from which today's page is taken. Nathan is sent by God to confront David. He tells David a story about a man whose actions make him deserving of death. Then Nathan points the finger at David and declares, "You are the man!" David finally makes a good decision. He gets honest with God and confesses, "I have sinned against the LORD." It begins the process of restoration. Confession is how we get honest with God. It requires taking time for self-examination, with an openness to the Holy Spirit. Take some time today to get away and honestly look inside to the places you are not being honest with yourself or God. 〰 *M*

Dear God, shine your light and truth through all the places inside where I try to hide. Heal me with your love. I am grateful for your love, your forgiveness, and your acceptance of me. Amen.

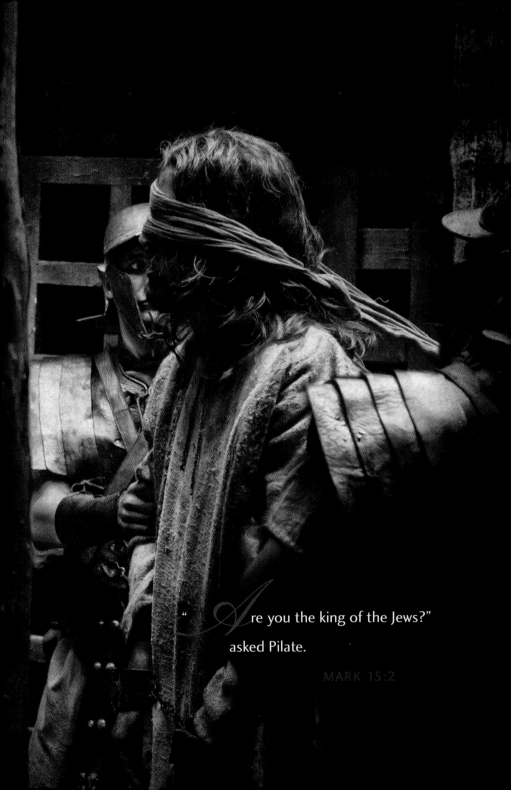

"Are you the king of the Jews?" asked Pilate.

MARK 15:2

Then Pilate announced to the chief priests and the crowd, "I find no basis for a charge against this man."

LUKE 23:4

"What shall I do, then, with Jesus who is called Christ?" Pilate asked.

MATTHEW 27:22

Create in me

a pure heart,

O God . . .

PSALM 51:10

We know the story of King David's debacle with Bathsheba and the prophet Nathan's confrontation of David's sin. In response, David got honest with God and confessed his sin. One outcome of his repentance was the composition of a song by David seeking restoration of his relationship with God. Today's verse is taken from that psalm.

Getting honest with God is the first step in restoring our relationship with God when we have blown it. The second step is seeking spiritual "cleansing." The image of getting clean permeates the Bible. Whether it was ceremonial washing at the Temple or the sacrament of baptism in the New Testament, we need spiritual cleansing.

In today's text, David prays for a pure or cleansed heart. He recognizes that this is something only God can do. We confess . . . he cleans. The idea of "pure" might be better translated as "purified." It refers to a heart that has gone through the fire and come out with a little more of its impurities removed. This will be a lifelong process. Without an ongoing experience of purification and cleansing, our spiritual lives will get bogged down in our fallen human nature.

Put a "C" on your hand today to remind you to echo David's great prayer. Let's ask God to keep cleansing our hearts. In the Sermon on the Mount, Jesus said that the payoff of having a purified heart is a deeper vision of God and a blessed life. I'd like to experience both on a more consistent basis. ✐ M

Father, purify my heart. I want to be honest and truthful with you. Let me experience your love again today. I want to be yours.
Amen.

Elijah said to her,
"Don't be
afraid. . . .
For this is
what the LORD,
the God of Israel,
says: 'The jar of
flour will not
be used up
and the jug
of oil will not
run dry until
the day the LORD
gives rain on
the land.'"

1 KINGS 17:13–14

Elijah was one of the greatest prophets of Israel. He spoke for God during the time of King Ahab, one of the most corrupt kings in Israel's history. Ahab's wife, Jezebel, was even more corrupt than he was. Elijah's message called Ahab and Jezebel to repentance. He was an instrument of God who was used to confront the evil that had spread throughout the land, before it was too late.

Today's text is a promise God gave a poor widow through Elijah. When Elijah met her, she only had flour and oil for one last meal for her and her son. She was about to cook that meal and then lie down and die! Elijah told her to use part of the flour and oil to make a small cake for him! Then he made this promise: if she would obey God, he would intervene miraculously, and the jar of flour and jug of oil would not be empty until the famine was over. She did what Elijah told her, and God did what he promised through Elijah.

When things look bleak, and you are at the end of your own resources, remember the widow. When we are in relationship with God and depend on him, he has resources and plans that are beyond our comprehension. He turns water into wine. He feeds thousands with a few fish and loaves. He works mysteriously so that flour and oil keep showing up in the jar. Our job is to make sure we are in the kind of relationship with him where he is able to lead us and provide for us. ✐ *RQM*

Father, in the same way you provided for Elijah, we ask you to meet our needs today. Keep us in the kind of relationship with you that will allow you to do the miraculous on our behalf. Thank you that even when our lives are stressed and strained, we can trust you. Amen.

Where is the wise man?
Where is the scholar?
Where is the philosopher of this age?
Has not God made foolish
the wisdom of the world?

1 CORINTHIANS 1:20

Many who no longer believe in God have been led to this position by thinking that faith is intellectually untenable. This is unfortunate. There have been some brilliant Christians in the history of the church. I think of people from my native England such as C. S. Lewis and J.R.R. Tolkien. I would match the intellect of these men against any of the men and women in recent times who have championed intellectual reasons for not believing in God.

The apostle Paul was brilliant. But, sometimes, as he wrote in today's verse, faith matters can seem foolish to some. A little later in the chapter from which today's verse is taken, Paul says there is a different kind of wisdom that God reveals in Christ. That which might seem foolish to some becomes marvelously wise when God opens the deeper parts of our being and reveals himself to us.

I consider myself a relatively intelligent person. I am usually smarter than a fifth grader! I believe in Jesus. Both Roma and I see the immense wisdom of how God has revealed his love through Christ and made it possible for us to have a relationship with him. It might seem foolish to some, but it makes perfect sense to us! *M*

Father, I will take your "foolishness"
over human "wisdom" any day.
Help me be a person who encourages
others to approach the Bible
with an open mind. Amen.

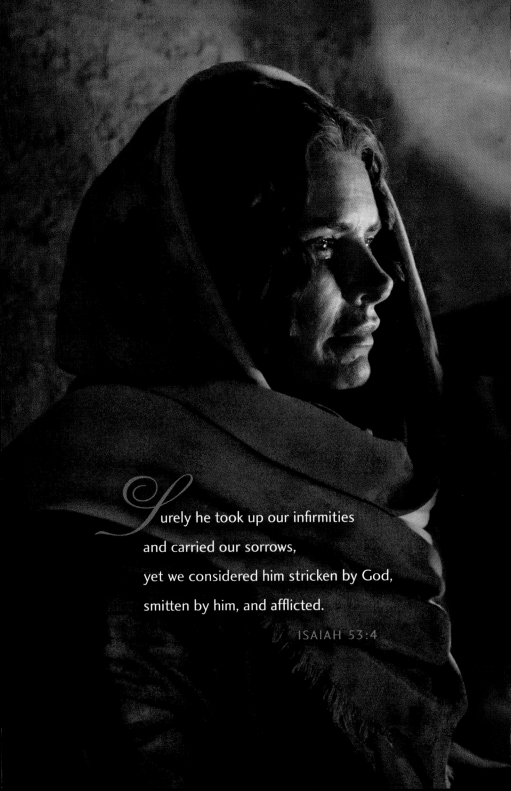

*Surely he took up our infirmities
and carried our sorrows,
yet we considered him stricken by God,
smitten by him, and afflicted.*

ISAIAH 53:4

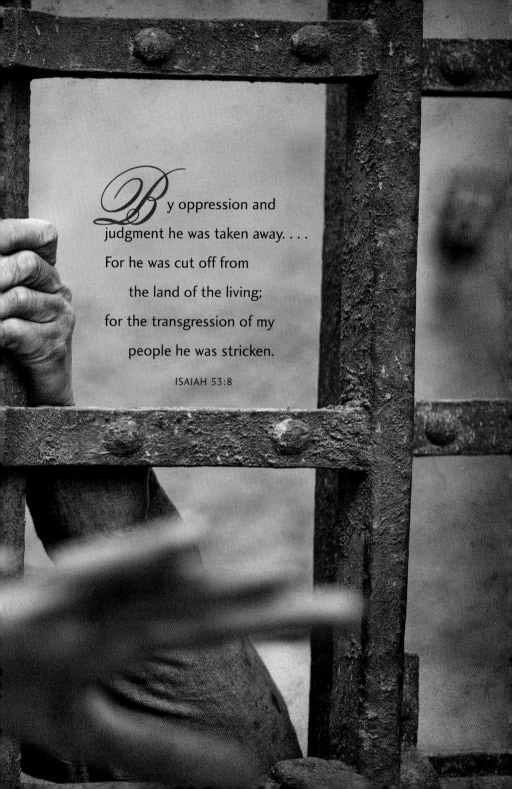

By oppression and judgment he was taken away. . . . For he was cut off from the land of the living; for the transgression of my people he was stricken.

ISAIAH 53:8

THE LORD SAID TO MOSES, . . .

"Then have them make

a sanctuary for me,

AND I WILL DWELL AMONG THEM."

EXODUS 25:1, 8

There is a common misunderstanding among many people that somehow the God of the Old Testament and the God of the New Testament are two different deities. The reasoning is based on a perspective that the Old Testament is all about wars, judgment, and God's vengeance, while the New is all about the love of God revealed in Jesus. Although it is understandable that some people could reach this conclusion, the fact is that the Old Testament is filled with great examples of the love of God. Today's verse is one of these.

God told Moses to have the Israelites build a sanctuary. It was called the Tabernacle. He told Moses that when it was built, he would dwell among them. This was to be a place where the sins of the people could be forgiven. This instruction was given immediately after Moses had been given God's Law on Mt. Sinai. You can think of it this way: the Law revealed the absolute moral standard that God expected the Israelites to follow in order to live in a proper relationship with him. The instructions for the Tabernacle revealed that God knew that the Israelites would struggle to meet that standard perfectly. Knowing this, he provided a means of forgiveness, because he is a loving God.

We call our home our "sanctuary." We know the moment we come home we are safe, because we have chosen to surround ourselves with God's love. While the dogs might bark sometimes, and it seems there is always a problem with the plumbing, our home is our sacred space—it is full of love, and we know God dwells there. Belief in God can make any space into a sanctuary. Open your heart to him today, and he will make your space a sanctuary. ✒ *R&M*

Father, we are so grateful that you love us, and we thank you that you offer it freely. Dwell in my space and help me to surround myself with your love. Work in my life today to help me live in a way that is pleasing to you. Amen.

> Trust in the LORD with all your heart and lean not on your own understanding.
> PROVERBS 3:5

When I was a little girl, I used to play a game with my friends, which was all about trust. One of us would stand with our back to the others. The others would promise to catch us. The person with their back to the others would then fall backward, trusting that their friends would be there. It was a little scary as you fell backward, not knowing if you would be caught or allowed to fall.

Today's verse is all about trust. The trust game is a good metaphor for what Solomon writes in this proverb. He tells us that we are to trust the Lord with all our hearts. It is probably the "all" that makes doing what he teaches difficult. I trust God. Mark and I have learned to trust him and depend upon him on a daily basis as we worked on *The Bible.* It hasn't always been easy. But God has always been faithful.

Sometimes in life, we find ourselves in situations where we are having a difficult time trusting God. Without realizing it, our lack of faith might be caused by what today's verse refers to as "leaning on our own understanding."

To lean on your own understanding is a metaphor for processing the events of our lives through the filters of our own perception and interpretation without including God. This approach to life can be unreliable. Trusting God doesn't mean that God wants us to stop thinking. But he wants to remind us that when we have carefully thought through situations and fully used the mental faculties he has given us, we are to run our human understanding through another filter to complete the picture. That filter is the unseen hand of God at work in our lives and all around us. ✍ *R*

Heavenly Father, thank you that we can trust you.
Help us trust you more completely, with all of our hearts.
When we have come to the end of our own resources,
remind us to trust you and your loving care for our lives.

"Do not let this Book of the Law depart from your mouth;
meditate on it day and night, so that you may
be careful to do everything written in it.
Then you will be prosperous and successful."

JOSHUA 1:8

Producing The Bible has been a life-changing experience. For three years of our lives, we have spent nearly every day immersed in the stories of the Bible. We also have tried to concentrate each day on one short passage of the Bible and think about it throughout the day. This is what today's verse refers to as "meditating" on the "Book of the Law." One reason we are writing this devotional book is so that you can experience what we have experienced by doing this. We hope that you will also be inspired.

In the start of episode 3 in *The Bible* series, we show the leadership of the nation of Israel passing from Moses to Joshua. It was at this very point in time that God spoke to Joshua, making the above promise. It is a promise of "prosperity" and "success." These words mean something quite different to God than they do to the world in which we live.

We have both been very blessed to have achieved success in our careers. But while we worked on this project, we have experienced a different kind of success and prosperity. It is the success of accomplishing something that God led us to do. And it is the prosperity of knowing that accomplishing the things God calls us to do results in a deep satisfaction and fulfillment that worldly success and prosperity can never bring.

We believe God wants your life to be prosperous and successful. He has plans for your life. Discovering and accomplishing them will involve reading and meditating on his Word—the Bible. We encourage you to reflect throughout the day on God's promise. *R@M*

Father, thank you for the gift of the Bible.
Thank you that you speak to us through it.
Thank you for your plans for our lives.
Help us today to discover those plans
and attempt to do them! All glory is yours.
Amen.

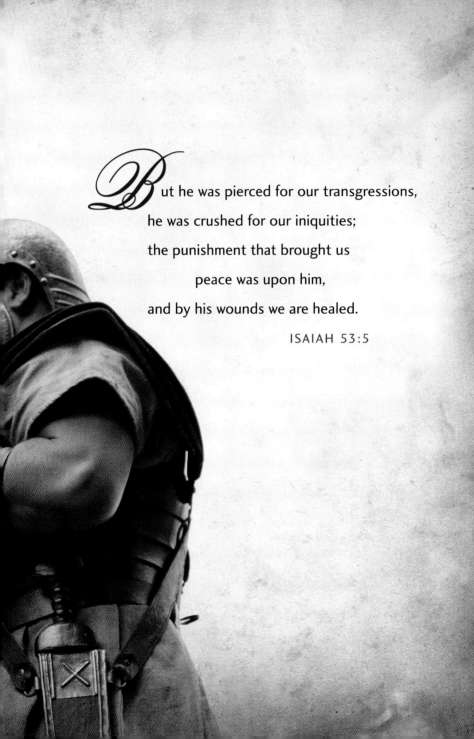

But he was pierced for our transgressions,

he was crushed for our iniquities;

the punishment that brought us

peace was upon him,

and by his wounds we are healed.

ISAIAH 53:5

Immediately Jesus

reached out his hand and caught him.

"You of little faith,"

he said, "why did you doubt?"

MATTHEW 14:31

*J*esus spoke the above words to a very wet disciple. We don't know the look on Jesus' face or the tone of his voice when he said it. We have a slight suspicion he might have had a smile on his face. Jesus had been taking a stroll across the Sea of Galilee. He was miraculously walking on the water! When the disciples first saw him, they were "terrified" and thought they were seeing a ghost. But from being terrified, Peter immediately went to the opposite extreme. He wanted to do what Jesus was doing. Jesus agreed to let him try.

In *The Bible* series, we see Peter actually climb out of the boat and take a few steps. But when his circumstances come crashing in, and the faith he had to step out of the boat turns to fear, he begins to sink and cries out to Jesus to save him. Jesus reaches out, catches Peter, and speaks today's verse to him.

When we hear the call of God in our lives and begin to seek his plans and purposes, the time will come when he will ask us to "get out of the boat." If we take the challenge, it is inevitable that we will face circumstances beyond our own capabilities. We will need to have faith.

We felt the call to make *The Bible* series. It was our time to "get out of the boat." There were times when we felt overwhelmed. In those moments, we held hands and prayed together. We asked the Lord to keep us from sinking. He was faithful.

Is there something in your life that you feel called to do? We would encourage you to "get out of the boat." A little faith is all you need. He will be there and reach out his hand to catch you. *R&M*

Father, following you is an adventure.
You call us to "get out of the boat" and trust you.
Help us keep our eyes on you and not on the waves.
We trust you and love you. Amen.

> In the beginning
> was the Word,
> and the Word
> was with God,
> and the Word
> was God.
>
> JOHN 1:1

Today's verse is the opening line of the gospel written by the apostle John. Twice in the Bible, the words "in the beginning" appear. They are the first words of the entire Bible, and they are the first words of the Gospel of John.

John walked with Jesus during the time of Jesus' ministry, and he was with Jesus at the end of the story on the island of Patmos. His character spans over sixty years on *The Bible* series.

As we planned the series, we decided we wanted to show how the story of the Bible comes full circle from the creation story of Genesis to the last words of Jesus in Revelation. We also wanted to show that from beginning to end, the story was about Jesus. Today's verse captures both of these objectives. John accomplished the first objective by using the opening words of the entire Bible to begin his story. And he used a critically important concept from his day to capture the second—he calls Jesus "the Word."

We love the significance of the language John chose in calling Jesus "the Word." We realize that this was John's way of communicating that Jesus was divine. It also was a way of telling people that Jesus was the source of meaning and purpose in life.

If you are looking for meaning and purpose in your life, we would encourage you to begin to read the words of John. They will point you to Jesus, and he can give you what you seek. ✍ *R&M*

Lord, we thank you that through Jesus our lives can have meaning and purpose. Thank you for all you have done and continue to do in our lives. Amen.

Praise the LORD, O my soul; all my inmost
being, praise his holy name. Praise the LORD,
O my soul, and forget not all his benefits.

PSALM 103:1–2

It is a good thing to periodically stop and think about all the good things God has done for us. If our response to God's goodness is anything like David's, we will be filled with gratitude and praise. In *The Bible*, we see David both as a young man and as an older king. He was far from perfect. But God said he was a man after his own heart (1 Samuel 13:14)! Part of what that means is that he loved to worship God.

David wrote today's verses about a thousand years before the time of Jesus. In the larger psalm, David reflects on many of the blessings and good things he has received from God, and then responds in praise.

The King James Version of the Bible so beautifully expresses these verses: "Bless the LORD, O my soul, and all that is within me, bless his holy name." A more modern version translates them: "Give thanks to the LORD, and never forget all he has done for you." These words are a great reminder of what we need to do on a regular basis.

In the psalm, David goes on to list six reasons why we should give God our praise: God forgives our sins; heals our illnesses; redeems us; loves us; gives us good things, and renews us. The final reason is metaphorically stated by David as, "your youth is renewed like the eagle's." How great is God! Just reading the verses makes us want to thank and praise him. ✍ *R@M*

Father, we praise you today. You have done so many
things for us that we don't even know where to
begin thanking you. Thank you for sending Jesus
so that we can be forgiven. Thank you for the times
we have prayed when sick and you have healed us.
Thank you for all the good gifts you have given us.
For all these things, we praise you and thank you
from the depths of our inmost being. Amen.

We all, like sheep, have gone astray,

each of us has turned to his own way;

and the LORD has laid on him

the iniquity of us all.

ISAIAH 53:6

. . . he was led like a lamb to the slaughter,

and as a sheep before her shearers is silent,

so he did not open his mouth.

ISAIAH 53:7

WHEN HE HAD RECEIVED THE DRINK,

Jesus said, "It is finished."

WITH THAT, HE BOWED HIS HEAD

and gave up his spirit.

JOHN 19:30

In John's account of the life of Christ, today's verse contains the final words Jesus spoke from the cross. John was there. We have felt from the beginning that *The Bible* project was a sacred trust. Nowhere did this feeling weigh more heavily than in recreating the crucifixion.

In episode 8, *The Bible* series shows Jesus being arrested late in the night before his death. During that night and into the early morning, he is subjected to a series of illegal trials by the religious establishment. We show him being taken to the Roman official in charge of Judea, Pontius Pilate. The Romans had taken away the right to use the death penalty from the Jews. Only the Romans themselves could execute a convict. Their primary means of capital punishment was one of the most brutal and painful ever invented: crucifixion.

Jesus' final cry from the cross was one of triumph. "It is finished." It means, "Paid in full." The cost of forgiveness and the penalty for the guilt that kept humanity from experiencing God's love had been "paid in full" by Jesus' sacrifice. What looked like tragic defeat was actually the greatest victory of all time. And the best was yet to come! ✍ *RⓄⓂ*

Heavenly Father, we are eternally grateful to you
for how you expressed your love for us in Jesus.
Lord, we can't tell you how grateful we are for what
you did for us on the cross. We will be thanking you
for all eternity that "It is finished!"
Amen.

> The only thing that counts is faith expressing itself through love.
>
> GALATIANS 5:6

We believe that the message of Jesus is very simple. Our faith in God is to be expressed through loving action. Today's verse is similar to Jesus telling the religious experts that loving God and loving your neighbor summarizes the entire Bible. This time it was St. Paul writing the message.

God gives us the great privilege of being instruments of his love. I learned this in a profound experience I had during the days I played Monica on *Touched by an Angel.*

It was almost Christmas, and I had gone to a children's hospital to spread some goodwill among children and parents who found themselves in the hospital at this time of year. As I was walking down the hallway, a group of parents and grandparents were coming out of a room. I realized from their immense sorrow that the child in the room had just died. I tried to get out of their way and give them the space they needed in this deeply profound moment. But the mother looked up and recognized me. She called me "Monica" and ran to me and threw her arms around me. I didn't know what to do.

She said she had prayed that God would send an angel, and here I was. Part of me wanted to say that I wasn't an angel; I just play one on television. But thankfully, I didn't say anything; I just held her. I held her lovingly and silently prayed for her. I wondered later if I had failed her. But my dear friend Della assured me that I had been an angel in that moment. At least I had been an instrument of God's love in a moment of great need. ᘑ *R*

Heavenly Father, we desire to be instruments of your love. Help us express our faith in you through loving those we meet along our path. Make us sensitive to the needs of those around us and use us as a blessing to others. Amen.

Suddenly their eyes were opened
and they recognized him.

LUKE 24:31

We are so grateful for the many ways God shows up for us. While in Morocco filming the series, we prayed every day that we would be guided, that we would be wise, and that we would make good decisions. Bringing the Bible to life on television brought with it a huge responsibility, and we prayerfully stepped into the call. And yet every corner we turned, every challenge we faced, and every obstacle we overcame, God was there—in small quiet ways, such as a gentle breeze on a hot day, and other times with such drama as thunder and rainstorms that forced us to shut down the production for a few hours. God showed up in unexpected and powerful moments, and we were grateful for the moments when we recognized him and felt safe and guided in his loving embrace.

When do you recognize God? Take a look today. He is everywhere—in the warm smile from a friend, the beauty of falling rain, maybe even that first sip of your morning coffee. When you look for him, he will be there. Wherever you arrive, he is already there lovingly waiting for you. Learn to open your eyes and see God in the details. He is everywhere. We are blessed. *R&M*

Dear Father, we know wherever we go, you are
already there. We pray that we will always recognize
you and appreciate how much you love us.
We love you. Thank you for always being there
for us. Keep us safe in the warmth of your embrace.
Amen.

_T_here was a written notice above him, which read:

THIS IS THE KING OF THE JEWS.

LUKE 23:38

After the suffering of his soul,

he will see the light of life and be satisfied;

by his knowledge my righteous

servant will justify many,

and he will bear their iniquities.

ISAIAH 53:11

Now this is what the LORD Almighty says:
"Give careful thought to your ways.
You have planted much, but have harvested little.
You eat, but never have enough.
You drink, but never have your fill.
You put on clothes, but are not warm.
You earn wages, only to put them
in a purse with holes in it."

HAGGAI 1:5–6

*T*he final scenes of the Old Testament segment of *The Bible* series (episode 5) show a remnant of the exiled children of Israel heading home to Jerusalem to rebuild their city and Temple. Today's verses are an exhortation to that same group of people, sixteen years later. Back in the land to rebuild the Temple, they had lost their sense of proper priorities. They had built their own homes, but the Temple was still in ruins.

God sent the prophet Haggai with one simple message: "Give careful thought to your ways!" Their fortunes had been reversed. Their crops weren't productive. Their basic needs were not being met. Their wages seemed to vanish like dust in the wind. Haggai told them why: they had drifted from making God their highest priority!

Many of us live our lives at a hectic pace. One of the dangers of modern society is that we spend so little time slowing down and evaluating whether we need to make some midcourse corrections. We rarely stop and give careful thought to our lives.

It is important to periodically evaluate where we are with God. Are we making him our highest priority? Have we placed our own interests and desires above his plans and purposes for our lives? If so, how is that working? Do we need to stop and make some corrections?

The Israelites did just that. They got back to work on the Temple. God began to bless them again, and he sent a new message through Haggai: "I am with you!" God is with us. *R@M*

Father, help us keep our priorities straight.
Help us keep you and your kingdom our greatest priority.
Help us take inventory of our spiritual lives
and get back on track. In Jesus' name. Amen.

But you, man of God, flee from all this, and pursue righteousness, godliness, faith, love, endurance and gentleness. Fight the good fight of the faith.

1 TIMOTHY 6:11–12

In episode 10 of *The Bible* series, we get an idea of what it might have been like to know the apostle Paul. He was a man who knew what was worth fighting for. He pursued his faith with immense focus and passion. Paul also was a great encourager to those who had come to faith in Jesus through his ministry. Timothy was one of these. The two had a very special relationship.

Today's verses come from a letter Paul wrote to Timothy. In them, Paul challenges Timothy to "fight the good fight." He uses the image of an ancient Olympic athlete who has to avoid certain things when he is training for the games and pursue certain things to win the contest. Unlike the Olympian, the things Paul tells Timothy to pursue to fight the "good fight of the faith" are character qualities.

Paul encourages Timothy to "pursue righteousness, godliness, faith, love, endurance and gentleness." These are the objectives that keep us in training for the "good fight." Think about focusing on one of these qualities each day, as if you were training for a fight. Monday could be "righteousness" day. Tuesday would be the day you do the "godliness" workout. After six days of striving to get in spiritual shape, Sunday will be your day of rest. A few months of "training" and you will be ready for the "ring."

Give the workout a try today. Ask the Holy Spirit, your internal "trainer," to work in your life to increase these qualities. Imagine yourself on that winning podium, and Jesus putting the gold around your neck and saying, "Well done, good and faithful servant!" *R@M*

Heavenly Father, we want to fight the good fight. We want our lives to be pleasing to you and effective for your kingdom. Help us avoid anything that would hinder this goal. Help us pursue the qualities that will help bring us closer to you. Amen.

*Then Samuel took a stone and set it up
between Mizpah and Shen. He named it Ebenezer,
saying, "Thus far has the LORD helped us."*

1 SAMUEL 7:12

When we first meet Samuel in episode 3 of *The Bible* series, he is an old man and is about to give Israel their first king. Samuel is the last of the judges and the first of the classic prophets. Today's verse is from an incident in Samuel's life when he was a younger man and had just seen the hand of God defeat the perennial enemy of Israel, the Philistines.

To honor God, Samuel set up a stone monument at the place of the victory. He called the stone, "Ebenezer." If you grew up in the church or attend a church that still sings the classic hymns, you might have sung the line from "Come Thou Fount of Every Blessing" that says, "Here I raise my Ebenezer." Most people sing the song without having any idea what the line means. It comes from today's text.

Ebenezer means "stone of help." Samuel had gathered the people of Israel at the city of Mizpah, about four miles northwest of Jerusalem. The Philistines heard about the meeting and marched on Samuel and the Israelites. Samuel cried out to the Lord for help, and God so confused the Philistines that the Israelites won the battle.

God wants to be our Ebenezer, our "stone of help." When we are in the right relationship with Christ, he is the source of our strength. Jesus even called the Holy Spirit "the Helper." However far we have come on our spiritual journey, it is all because God has brought us "thus far." He is the one who will take us the rest of the way. Along the way, when battles are won, we need to raise a spiritual "Ebenezer" of praise and thanksgiving. M

Heavenly Father, you are our rock. You are the one who gives us help against all the things in the world that keep us from being all you created us to be. Thank you that we can call on you as Samuel did, and we know you will hear us. In Jesus' name. Amen.

GRACE AND PEACE TO YOU

from God our Father

and the Lord Jesus Christ.

PHILIPPIANS 1:2

In episode 10 of *The Bible* series, we tell the story of Saul, the Jewish Pharisee, becoming Paul, the Christian evangelist. Paul was a man God used to change the world. The New Testament is a compilation of twenty-seven individual documents. The apostle Paul wrote thirteen of these letters. Today's verse is taken from one of these letters.

Paul usually began his letters with a blessing. Today's verse comes from his letter to the Christians in the Roman city of Philippi. Paul "sends" them God's grace and peace in his blessing. God wants you to experience both. The root idea of *grace* is the concept of a gift. Christian faith is based on the reality that God gives us grace. We don't earn it. It is a gift made possible by what Jesus did on the cross. But grace is more than a concept; it is a spiritual reality. We can experience God's grace. It is offered as a gift. All we have to do is receive it. We can't earn it or buy it, but we can experience it.

Peace in the Bible is much more than the end of hostility. God's peace produces a state of total well-being that includes spiritual harmony with God, relational harmony between people, physical health, material provision, and an inner state of serenity. It is the product of living in a right relationship with God. In some traditions, when believers come together, they "share the peace." People turn to one another and bless one another by saying, "the peace of Christ be with you." Today, it is our hope that when you read these words, may you experience grace and peace from God the Father and the Lord Jesus Christ!

Father, thank you for your grace given to us
through Jesus Christ. We know that when we are
in a relationship with you, we can experience your peace.
We ask that you would touch our lives
with your grace and peace today. Amen.

A week later his disciples were in the house again,

and Thomas was with them.

Though the doors were locked,

Jesus came and stood among them and said,

"Peace be with you!"

JOHN 20:26

"*I* am the resurrection and the life.
He who believes in me will live,
even though he dies."

JOHN 11:25

"I am the LORD your God, who brought you out of Egypt, out of the land of slavery. You shall have no other gods before me."

EXODUS 20:2–3

There are so many great moments in Moses' life that we had a difficult time choosing which ones to include in *The Bible* series. Today's verses are taken from a moment we knew we had to film in episode 2.

As the newly freed Israelites camped at the foot of Mt. Sinai, Moses climbed the mountain where he first encountered God. In his first encounter, God appeared to Moses in the burning bush and gave him the commission to return to Egypt and lead the Exodus. In this encounter, God gives Moses a moral compass to guide the Israelites as his special nation. These Ten Commandments have shaped the history of the Western world.

The first commandment of the ten provides the overriding dynamic by which man and God are to relate to one another. If we want to have a loving relationship with God, we need to let God be God.

"You shall have no other gods before me" is not suggesting that other real gods exist. God is saying that when anything in our lives becomes more important than our relationship with him, it has become a "god."

Every now and then it is important to stop and ask the question, "Who is God in my life?" If the answer is anything other than God, it gives us a chance to get him back where he belongs, in the center of our lives. *R@M*

Father, thank you today that you are truly God. I desire for you to be the most important person in my life today. Show me if anything has taken the place that only you are worthy to hold. Help me love you and experience your love.

*If you fully obey the LORD your God and carefully
follow all his commands I give you today,
the LORD your God will set you high above all
the nations on earth. All these blessings
will come upon you and accompany you
if you obey the LORD your God.*

DEUTERONOMY 28:1–2

After forty years of wandering in the wilderness, the Israelites were about to enter the Promised Land. But it was a new generation that would cross the Jordan. Only three men who were over the age of twenty when the Jews left Egypt remained. One was Moses, and he would not enter the land with the people. He did set eyes on the Promised Land, but died on Mt. Nebo, never to enter it. Today's verses are part of his final message to the children of Israel.

God desired to bless the Israelites in the Promised Land. But in the chapters that follow this promise of blessing, Moses tells the people what will happen if they turn their backs on God. He warns them of the serious consequences of disobedience. What you see in *The Bible* series is what happened when the nation turned from God, and for the next five hundred years of their history they experienced a roller-coaster ride of periods of blessing followed by years of conquest and devastation.

God desires to bless you. He has instructed us in the Bible how to live in a way that maximizes his blessing. If we open our lives to him and seek his blessing, he will give it. Then as we live according to his instructions, our lives will be further blessed. *RAM*

Father, we pray today that you would help us
live in a way that we can experience your blessing.
We open our lives to you. Live in us and through us,
we pray. Amen.

"But a Samaritan, as he traveled,

came where the man was;

and when he saw him,

he took pity on him."

LUKE 10:33

Today's verse comes from one of our favorite stories of Jesus. It is a story of kindness.

The Samaritans were disliked. They were avoided at all cost and treated as if they were subhuman. This background helps us understand why Jesus' story had such an impact on his audience. Purely from a story perspective, it contains another one of those brilliant twists that made the art of Jesus' storytelling brilliant. As Jesus tells it in the parable, he shows the Samaritan as the hero and his own people as the bad guys. This took a lot of guts! We like that about Jesus. He never pulled punches.

Reading this parable is a good reminder to all of us that if we ever find ourselves in a situation where someone is in need that we don't pass by on the other side. It doesn't matter whether the person is "like me" or "not." It is important to do the right thing and step up.

Father, make us more like the Good Samaritan. Increase the measure of kindness and caring in our lives. Help us judge less and help more. Only you can change our hearts. Work in us today. Thank you. Amen.

Jesus answered,
"I am the way
and the truth
and the life. No
one comes to
the Father except
through me."

JOHN 14:6

In The Bible series, there is a powerful scene in the Upper Room where Jesus speaks the words of today's verse to his disciples. Throughout history, there have been many religious leaders and philosophers who have said, "This is the way." Only Jesus said, "I AM the way."

In the context, Jesus had just been telling his friends that he was "going away." He said that they knew the way to where he was going. Of course, they really didn't have a clue where he was going or the way to get there. Only Thomas was honest enough to admit it. It was in response to this admission that Jesus spoke these words.

Jesus is the way. In the ultimate sense, he was speaking about going to be with the Father. We call that place heaven. Jesus says that getting there is not a matter of what you do; it is a matter of understanding that Jesus himself *is* the way.

Jesus is the truth. Truth does not only consist of accurate information. Jesus embodied truth. He spoke the truth. He lived the truth. He is the truth.

Jesus is the life. As Jesus told Nicodemus, everyone needs to be born of the Spirit. Jesus gave his life so that we could have life. Spiritual life is found in him. The apostle John will later write: "He who has the Son has life" (1 John 5:12).

When we open our lives and invite him to come into our hearts, we possess the way, the truth, and the life. ✒ *RQM*

Lord Jesus, I believe in you. I believe you are the way, the truth, and the life. I open my life to you. Come and live in me. Make me the person you created me to be. In your name I pray. Amen.

"For I know the plans I have for you,"
declares the LORD, *"plans to prosper you*
and not to harm you, plans to give you
hope and a future."

JEREMIAH 29:11

We like to think that there is a personal application for this verse in our personal lives. God has plans for us that he has been working out all our lives. They have a present and a future dimension. "What has God been preparing you all your life to do?" We're at a point in life where many of our friends are slowing down, but we are just getting going! Years of hard work have resulted in a number of current hit series—*Survivor, Apprentice, Are You Smarter Than a Fifth Grader? Shark Tank*, and, of course, *The Voice*. But instead of taking it easy, Roma and I took on our most ambitious and difficult series ever, *The Bible*. It took us three years to produce it and was at times exhausting, challenging, and difficult. But it has always been worth it. We felt called to do it, and we love it.

Abraham was seventy-five when God called him to his life work. Moses was eighty! We have to believe that in both cases God had used the entirety of their life experiences to prepare them for his call.

Some of you are young and just getting started in your adult life. God has plans for you. They are good plans. He wants to bless and prosper you. Some of you are more "mature." Don't think God is finished with you. You will know when that day arrives. Be encouraged today. Seek first the kingdom. Put a "P" on your hand to remind you of God's plans for you! *M*

Dear God, we know you have a plan for our lives.
Give us the strength to do as you wish
and to be inspired by you. We are ready
and willing to be in your service. We are yours.
Amen.

THEN JESUS CAME TO THEM AND SAID,
"All authority in heaven and on earth
has been given to me. Therefore go
and make disciples of all nations,
baptizing them in the name of
the Father and of the Son and of
the Holy Spirit, and teaching them
to obey everything I have commanded you.
AND SURELY I AM WITH YOU ALWAYS,
to the very end of the age."

MATTHEW 28:18–20

Today's verses are the last recorded words of Jesus in Matthew's account of his life. They have come to be known as "The Great Commission." Usually, these verses are read in the context of telling the world about Jesus. Sometimes, the last few words might get overlooked, and yet they are more important than the commission in which they are found. Jesus promises, "I am with you always, to the very end of the age."

Every day, every minute, every second, Jesus is with us. We might not be aware of his presence. We might not even *believe* he is present. But that doesn't change the fact that he is. He is with you! This is *always* true!

Times were coming when the disciples would experience trials in their lives when they probably wondered, *Where is Jesus?* We dramatized some of these moments in the final hour of episode 10 of *The Bible*. We show the great faith of those disciples to think back and remember these words.

We have always loved the words of "Footprints in the Sand." It is the beautiful story of a person walking down a beach and seeing their life represented by two sets of footprints: theirs and the Lord's. Periodically, the two sets would become one. It always seemed to happen at the most difficult times in their life. The writer asks Jesus, "Did you leave me in these times?" Jesus replies, "No, I carried you!" *R&M*

Heavenly Father, thank you that you will
never leave us or forsake us. Help us know
that even when we don't feel your presence, you are here.
Help us remember that even when we don't feel your love,
you still love us. Amen.

> We all, like sheep, have gone astray, each of us has turned to his own way; and the LORD has laid on him the iniquity of us all.
>
> ISAIAH 53:6

We are always amazed at the relentless love of God. During the filming of *The Bible*, we were struck by this sense that again and again and again, God gave his people another chance. People failed, but God was faithful.

We love this verse in Isaiah. It captures the sense that even though we have turned away from God, he will never turn away from us. While we were filming the series, there were often sheep and shepherds near the set. Watching them keep their sheep together reminded me of the old saying, "It is like herding cats!" We imagine this is a good image of what the history of humanity looks like through the eyes of God.

The scenes of Jesus on the cross in *The Bible* series are very emotional and extraordinarily moving. Filming those scenes gave us an entirely new sense of the immense nature of God's love for us. Even though we were only filming a TV series, everyone on the set found the scenes gut-wrenching. We will never think about the crucifixion in the same way. It was as though God was calling out to the entire universe, "Here is how much I love you!" Let that love strengthen you today. *R@M*

Father, thank you that you love me. If not for your love, I would be lost. Thank you for what Jesus did for me on the cross. Thank you for forgiveness and the ability to experience your love. Help me feel your presence and love today and every day. Amen.

The angel said to the women, "Do not be afraid,
for I know that you are looking for Jesus,
who was crucified. He is not here;
he has risen, just as he said.
Come and see the place where he lay."

MATTHEW 28:5–6

The resurrection of Christ is the most important event in human history. Everything Jesus claimed about himself, and what he foretold he would accomplish on the cross, rested on whether or not he would be raised from the dead.

Today's verses were spoken to two women, Mary Magdalene and another unnamed woman, who came to the tomb that first Easter morning. When they arrived, the Roman guard that had been placed there to guard the tomb was gone. The stone that sealed the tomb had been rolled away. Sitting on the stone was an angel, whose appearance had frightened away some of the toughest soldiers on the planet and now terrified the two women. But they had nothing to fear. This angel was there to give them the greatest message in human history: "He has risen!" Jesus Christ had conquered death!

The women looked inside the tomb. Where once a body had lain, now only empty grave clothes remained. Someone has observed that the angel didn't roll the stone away to let Jesus out, but to let the disciples in. For Jesus wasn't gone, he was back! He had risen from the dead! As the text tells us, "Just as he said."

Jesus is alive! This is the message of the good news: the Gospel. Because he lives, he can be a part of our lives. We can be forgiven and experience new life when we open our hearts and invite Jesus to come live in us. *RQM*

Father, thank you that Christ is risen!
Thank you that death could not hold him.
Lord Jesus, you are alive! You have told us
that if we would open our lives to you,
you would come and live in us.
Come, Lord Jesus. Live in me. Amen.

*J*esus answered, "I am the way
and the truth and the life.
No one comes to the Father
except through me."

JOHN 14:6

DAY 92

"But store up for yourselves treasures in heaven,
where moth and rust do not destroy,
and where thieves do not break in and steal.
For where your treasure is,
there your heart will be also."

MATTHEW 6:20–21

*D*o you ever worry about how your personal investments are doing? If you have invested in the stock market, you never know day-to-day whether you are going to gain ground or lose ground. In recent times, people have lost their entire life savings in a single day. Investing in the world is risky business.

Jesus talks about another kind of investment in today's verses. When you invest in God's kingdom, you always know you are going to get a great return. It is guaranteed!

Immediately before today's verses, Jesus talked about bad investments. He used the concept of "storing up treasures" on earth. Putting all your eggs in the basket of the things our culture tells us are important is a bad investment. Later in the passage, Jesus referred to this investment strategy as "serving Money," or *Mammon*—a word that was personified in the text, but generally referred to monetary wealth.

According to Jesus, good investments involve "storing up treasures" in heaven. With the greatest insider information possible, Jesus guarantees that these investments will never fail. They will always give you a good return on investment.

In Jesus' day, it was understood that acts of kindness and gifts given for kingdom purposes were heavenly investments. Maybe it is time for us to review our "investment portfolio." We might need to shift some of our investments from treasures on earth to treasures in heaven.

The big message of today's verses is, "where your treasure is, there your heart will be also." ✍ *RQM*

Father, help us today to take stock of where our treasure truly is. Help us have good hearts that invest in kindness, mercy, and generosity. We want our hearts to be set on heavenly things, not purely earthly ones. We need your help to change our hearts. In Jesus' name we pray. Amen.

> Because of the LORD's great love we are not consumed, for his compassions never fail. They are new every morning; great is your faithfulness.
>
> LAMENTATIONS 3:22–23

One of the most violent scenes in *The Bible* takes place at the end of the Old Testament portion of the series (episode 5). We portray the repeated warnings of the prophet Jeremiah to Zedekiah, the last king of Judah. With Zedekiah's refusal to respond to God's warning, the Babylonians lay siege to the city and destroy it. Today's verses come from a lament Jeremiah wrote as he saw the city in flames and the Temple of God destroyed.

As a younger man, I served in the military, and Roma grew up in the "troubles" of Northern Ireland. We have both seen and experienced the horror of war. I can almost imagine Jeremiah looking around at the devastation war has wrought and wondering what he might say. Then out of his mouth came these words: "Because of the LORD's great love, we are not consumed, for his compassions never fail. They are new every morning; great is your faithfulness." In the midst of devastation, Jeremiah remembers God's faithfulness. Seventy years will pass, but God will give Israel another chance. There is hope.

We have found this to be true in our lives. God is faithful. There is always hope. As we produced the series, we had a growing realization of how the Old Testament is a record of repeated unfaithfulness on the part of the people God had called to himself. At times God used the forces of history to discipline and correct them. But he was always faithful. He repeatedly gave them new chances. Ultimately, that faithfulness found its full expression in Jesus Christ. Through Jesus we find forgiveness and a new start.

You might feel that your life is a wreck today. Perhaps Jerusalem going up in flames is a good image of how you feel. Your circumstances might seem bleak. But take today's verses to heart. God loves you. He is faithful. There is hope. *R@M*

Father, we thank you today for your love and faithfulness. Because of your love, we have hope. Great is your faithfulness. We love you with all our hearts. Amen.

*After his suffering, he presented himself
to these men and gave many convincing
proofs that he was alive. He appeared
to them over a period of forty days
and spoke about the kingdom of God.*

ACTS 1:3

From the beginning, when we started on *The Bible* series, we knew that we wanted to include the resurrection. Yes, we would show the cross, but it did not end there. We were committed to not only make sure the resurrection was part of the series, but that we also showed Jesus during the days after the resurrection all the way to his appearance to John on the island of Patmos. These scenes appear in episode 10 of our series.

As we filmed the life of Christ, we often had the sense that God was present with us. Because of the resurrection, Jesus is not just a dead religious figure. He is alive and real today. Good Friday was not the end of the story. Easter was not the end of the story. The Ascension was not the end of the story. Not even Jesus' visit to John on Patmos was the end of the story. We are part of the story. Today is part of the story. It is a story of God and all of us. ✍ *RMM*

Lord Jesus, I'm glad that you are alive.
You promised that if we would open our hearts
to you, you would come and live in us by
your Spirit. I need you today. Come and live
in and through me today and every day. Amen.

SAVE ME, O GOD,

for the waters have

come up to my neck.

PSALM 69:1

In *The Bible* series, we show that King David of Israel went through some tough stretches in his life. Today's verse comes from a psalm David wrote when he was feeling overwhelmed by his problems. He uses the metaphor of "waters" to refer to his situation. His expression "the waters have come up to my neck" reminds us that we are "up to our necks in alligators." When we are feeling that way, we need to remember David!

David uses a few other choice expressions to further voice his complaint: "I sink in the miry depths," "The floods engulf me," "I am worn out calling for help," "People make sport of me," "I am scorned, disgraced, and shamed," and "I am in pain and distress." We don't know exactly what was going on with David, but we know that on some days and in some ways we can probably all relate.

Given the outpouring of difficulties David expresses, it is amazing that the psalm has an upbeat ending. He cries out that God would "save" him. Later in the psalm, we see David's great confidence that God is going to answer that prayer for help. We also see how the psalm has a connection to Jesus.

This psalm is prophetic. In episode 7 of *The Bible* series, we portray the incident at the Temple when Jesus turned over the tables of the moneychangers. When John tells the story in his gospel, he quotes a verse from this psalm: "Zeal for your house will consume me" (John 2:17). The psalm also contains the prophetic words: "they gave me gall for my food, and vinegar for my thirst." The entire psalm is a reminder that Jesus understands when we feel overwhelmed. I hope you are not having a day where you can relate to this verse too much. But if you are, or when you do, this is a good one to remember. ✑ *RⒶM*

Lord Jesus, you understand when we feel as though
the difficulties of life are about to take us under.
You always answer when we pray, "Save me, O God."
Thank you that you love me and care about me. Amen.

> The heavens declare the glory of God; the skies proclaim the work of his hands.
>
> PSALM 19:1

How beautifully the psalmist captures the image of the presence of God revealed in his creation! As I look out over the ocean from our home, I feel so blessed. I feel the presence of God everywhere. God desires to speak to us through nature. The Bible itself says this in today's verse. This reality has played a significant role in my own spiritual life.

I try to take time in the morning to read the Bible and pray. I often hike in the hills or go down to the beach and spend time walking beside the ocean. I am always reminded of the vastness of God and that His love for us is as wide as the ocean, as high as a mountain, and as deep as the sea. I pray and tell God how much I love him. I feel his love expand in my heart.

When we finished filming *The Bible* in Morocco, we took a few days to unwind. We left Morocco very exhausted. We both had a desire to get to higher ground as a symbol of completing the filming of the series. We ended up in Switzerland, climbing to the base of the Matterhorn together.

We stood hand and hand, giving thanks to God that we had made it through the shoot safely, that none of our cast and crew were seriously injured, and that we had captured beautiful footage that would honor and glorify God. We stood in the grandeur of the mountains, expressing gratitude in our hearts. The mountains framed us in a way that gave me the sense that we were in nature's cathedral. The presence of God was very real.

We are blessed to have access to these spectacular places where we have experienced God's presence in nature. I hope you have a place near you that enables you to enjoy the same. If you do, I encourage you to go to your "cathedral" and seek God. Be still. He will be there with you. *R*

Heavenly Father, we thank you that you speak to us. You speak through the Bible. You speak to our hearts in prayer. You speak through the beauty and grandeur of your creation. Remind us today to look for you all around us. Help us experience your love today. In your name we pray. Amen.

I turned around to see the voice that was speaking to me. And when I turned I saw seven golden lampstands, and among the lampstands was someone "like a son of man," dressed in a robe reaching down to his feet and with a golden sash around his chest.

REVELATION 1:12–13

The Bible series ends with the risen and glorified Christ appearing to the apostle John on the island of Patmos. Today's verses give us a glimpse of what John experienced. They were written at the end of the first century when John was quite elderly. It was a difficult time for the early followers of Jesus. They were being persecuted by the Roman Empire. John himself had been sent to Patmos to work as a slave in the Roman mines for which the island was infamous. We show this sequence in episode 10 of the series.

In the midst of a difficult and discouraging situation, John hears a voice speaking to him. He turns to see who is speaking and sees Jesus. John had spent three years with Jesus before the crucifixion. He had been with Jesus for forty days after the resurrection. But the Jesus whom John now encounters on Patmos is different. Jesus now possesses the glory that he willingly laid aside in the incarnation. He is no longer the "Suffering Servant" of Isaiah's prophecies. He is now the "Conquering King" of Daniel's visions. Note John's response.

Jesus brings John a message of hope and encouragement. He affirms that he is coming again. When he comes, all that is wrong will be made right. It is a message that has encouraged Christians throughout the ages. May this same message bring you hope and encouragement today. *ROM*

Lord, we all have problems and pain. We see horrible things happen, and we find it confusing. In those times, help us remember how you revealed yourself to John. Remind us that a day is coming when you will wipe every tear from our eyes. Remind us that on that day, all will be well. Amen.

"He will wipe every tear from their eyes.

There will be no more death

or mourning or crying or pain,

for the old order of things has passed away."

REVELATION 21:4

*T*he final chapters of the book of Revelation bring the story of the Bible to an amazing conclusion. From the moment of creation, God has been working out a plan. In the final episode of *The Bible* series, we show how the risen and glorified Christ appeared to John on the island of Patmos and gave John a vision of how the story ends.

God has something planned for us that is beyond our capacity to fully comprehend. The images of the last few chapters of Revelation give us a hint of what is to come. Many think that when Jesus returns he will restore the beauty that existed before the Fall. But the vision Jesus gave John implies that the future is going to be infinitely more wonderful than Eden.

Today's verses tell us that part of Jesus making everything new means a day is coming when every tear will be wiped from our eyes. All the things that cause pain, grief, and death will cease to exist. As John was told, "the old order of things" will pass away, and a new order will come into being.

Sometimes these promises seem far off and hard to apply to our daily lives. We live between the resurrection and the return of Christ. But when things are hard, God wants us to know that as sure as Jesus came once, he is coming again. When we understand what God has promised, it gives us hope. *R&M*

Father, thank you that you have shown us that a day
is coming when the old order will pass away
and all things will be made new.
Help us live with that hope today. Amen.

> The Spirit and the bride say, "Come!" And let him who hears say, "Come!" Whoever is thirsty, let him come; and whoever wishes, let him take the free gift of the water of life.
>
> REVELATION 22:17

As we come to the end of these devotional thoughts, it seemed appropriate to go to the end of the story. *The Bible* series ends with Jesus appearing to John on the island of Patmos. Jesus gives John a revelation of the things that are yet to come. The last chapter of the Bible ends with an invitation from Jesus. Today's verse contains that invitation.

Jesus extends an invitation to anyone who is willing to "Come!" It is an invitation to enter into a relationship with him and all the Bible promises to those who open themselves to the love of God. In context, this invitation occurs shortly after the risen Christ has shown John a vision of the coming kingdom and the New Jerusalem.

The tree of life that was removed from humanity's access in Genesis is now present in this new city. Adam and Eve picked the wrong tree. It led to death. Because of Jesus, we will be able to eat from the "right" tree. The fruit of this tree is eternal life!

A river runs through the New Jerusalem. It is called "the river of the water of life." This river contains immediate and unlimited access to the Holy Spirit. Jesus says, "Whoever wishes, let him take the free gift of the water of life."

From beginning to end, the Bible is an invitation from God to come back to him. He loves you. He loves us all. Open your heart to him today.

RAM

Heavenly Father, we thank you that the message you want us to hear is one of your love. We hear it. Keep us daily turning to you and opening our hearts so we can experience your love. Use us as instruments of your love in the lives of all you bring across our path. In your name we pray. Amen.

"Yes, I am coming soon." Amen.
Come, Lord Jesus. The grace of the Lord Jesus
be with God's people. Amen.

REVELATION 22:20–21

We shot the very last scene of *The Bible* series on the very last day of filming. If you have worked on a production such as this, you know the chances of that happening are extraordinary. Films are never shot sequentially, so this was a truly rare moment.

It was a day of mixed feelings for us. We had all worked so hard to bring it to this point, and we had poured our hearts into it. We were looking forward to getting home after four months on location, but we were sad for it to end. We felt that we had been called to make this series, and we had prayerfully brought it to completion with God's help on this final day. We were shooting on a beautiful mountain location overlooking the water. The setting was Patmos, and the scene was Jesus showing up in John's vision in Revelation (episode 10 of our series). A few of us stepped off to the side to pray as we had done so many times on the set. Jesus said, "For where two or three come together in my name, there I am with them" (Matthew 18:20), and as we prayed we felt the Lord was with us. This prayer was a prayer of gratitude that he had been with us and had brought us through, that with his help we had completed filming.

Our prayer remains that this series will be a blessing to others and that through watching this series more people will read the Bible. We hope that the series and this book will go out into the world and bless and inspire others, ultimately bringing them closer to God. This final scene is full of the promise of hope for all of us. May the grace of the Lord Jesus be with God's people. *R@M*

Dear Lord Jesus, thank you for being there and showing up for us. Thank you for being a blessing to us. Breathe your love into us that we may be more like you. Fill us with your Holy Spirit that we may step into our future strengthened by your grace and empowered by your love. The message you want us to hear is love. Let us hear it today and every day. May the grace of our Lord Jesus be with all God's people. Amen.

"Yes, I am coming soon." Amen. Come, Lord Jesus. The grace of the Lord Jesus be with God's people. Amen.

REVELATION 22:20–21

We hope this book has been a blessing to your life.

If so, we invite you to read our novel

A Story of God and All of Us.

It, too, is based on the epic TV

miniseries *The Bible* and is

available wherever books are sold.